THE

SCIENCE

OF

CYBERSECURITY

ALAN RADLEY

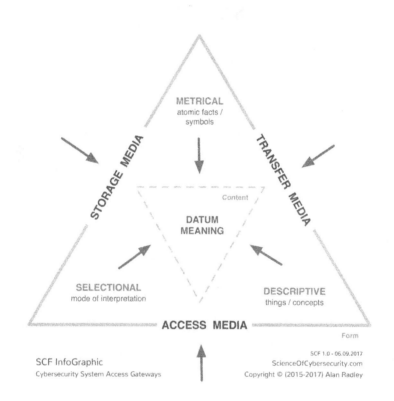

METRICAL
atomic facts /
symbols

STORAGE MEDIA

TRANSFER MEDIA

Content

DATUM
MEANING

SELECTIONAL
mode of interpretation

DESCRIPTIVE
things / concepts

ACCESS MEDIA

Form

SCF InfoGraphic
Cybersecurity System Access Gateways

SCF 1.0 - 06.09.2017
ScienceOfCybersecurity.com
Copyright © (2015-2017) Alan Radley

THE

Science

Of

Cybersecurity

A

TREATISE ON

COMMUNICATIONS SECURITY

By

Alan Radley

RADLEY
BOOKS

2018

for Mum and Dad

and dedicated to:

Kim, Francisco, Restie and Rowena,

Ruth, Chris, Nigel Pugh and

Philip, Ellen, Nigel, Arlene, Joshua,

Emma, Ben, and Caroline Radley.

Virtual Copies (Free)

On the website links given below, the author provides the reader with one free virtual copy of the complete contents of this book (PDF format); and also virtual copies for each figure/diagram presented here (PDF and PNG formats); however said copies are strictly for individual/personal use, and the author retains all rights to said copies as protected by international copyright law(s).

www.alanradley.com

www.scienceofcybersecurity.com

CONTENTS

Acknowledgments

THE AUTHOR acknowledges all of the friends, mentors, writers, teachers and others who took the time to time to impart various nuggets of wisdom. Full copyright is acknowledged (where known) for all works, and quoted in the list of captions or else the original publication is given or else the publication date is provided wherever possible.

Especial thanks to Professor Kim Veltman, Professor Francisco V. Cipolla-Ficarra, Dr Ted Nelson, Dave and Rose Gentle, Restie and Rowena Wight, Philip, Ellen, Nigel, Arlene, Joshua, Emma, Ben, and Caroline Radley, Nigel Pugh, Clark Hood, Ruth Grundy, Chris Green and others. Heartfelt thanks to Ruth Grundy, Chris Green, Nigel Pugh, Bill Montgomery, Frank Rowland, Vic Hyder, Ross Johnson, Richard Vizor, Michael Krausz, Julian Cordingley, Eugene Panferov, Christian Rogan, Vitali Kremez, Professor John Walker, Sean McGurk, Ahmed W, Troels Oerting, Kent Schramm, Peter E. Sand, Dr Merrick S. Watchorn, Richard Stiennon, Daniel McGarvey, Bruce Roberts, Ricardo Baretzky, Kevin T. McDonald, Jim O'Conner, Jonathan Trull, Marcus H. Sachs, Subrahmanya Gupra Boda, Ross Johnson, Sunil Varkey, David Jordan, Pantazis Kourtis, Benoit Piton, Graham Thompson, Martin Lee, Utkarsh Sinha, Dr Rizwan Ahmad, Laszlo Dellei, Ratan Jyoti, Tony Robinson, Ido Naor, Anthony Scarola, Stuart Naisbett, Anand R. Prasad, Kevin Hickey, Allan Watt, Jonathan Coombes, David Marugan, Dave Brown, Martin Visser, Michael Lester, Paul Kearney, Michael Hopkins, Cedric Thevenet, Colonel John Doody, Paul Crespo, Richard Redditt, Alex Smirnoff, Patric J.M. Versteeg, Christophe Duhamel, Arno Brok, Peter Bassill, Carl Landwehr, Adam Shostack, Roy Maxion, Dusko Pavlovic, Fred Schneider, Ged Austen, Tim Burnett, Sanjay Basu, Bobby Woodard, Bradley Rotter, Tony Collings (OBE) and Professor Richard Benham for reading/correcting/inspiring and discussing the manuscript—and for supplying expert advice/support plus inspiration.

Author's Credentials

ALAN RADLEY is a writer, inventor and generalist/technologist who is based in the UK. Alan holds a Bachelor's degree in Astronomy, and also a Doctor of Philosophy (Ph.D.) degree in Physics (from University College London); plus he has two Master's degrees: one in Spacecraft Technology and another in Business Administration. He has worked as a research fellow at University College London and as a senior research scientist for the European Space Agency and NASA. Alan is a regular public and keynote speaker, and he has taught over 500 students on undergraduate and postgraduate courses in physics, astronomy and computing.

Alan has written 10 books himself, and he has been co-editor and co-author of 5 Handbooks on Computing published by Blue Herons Press. Alan is on the editorial advisory board for the AInCI Computing Handbooks; and is the author of 10 papers in this series; the latter being for the International Association of Interactive Communication (AInCI); where he has been on the scientific committees for 12 international conferences, workshops and symposia held/planned in Rome, Venice, Toronto, Madrid etc between 2013-2017.

CHAPTER I

Introduction

OUR GOAL is to establish Cybersecurity as a science.

But if Cybersecurity is—in actual fact—a science, or could potentially be established as a science, then we must ask—what kind of a science is Cybersecurity?

In his article: '*Cybersecurity; From Engineering To Science*', Dr Carl Landwehr asked a related question: "*What would a scientific foundation for a Cybersecurity Science look like?*" [1,2].

It is salient to quote from Dr Landwehr's article:

> Science can come in several forms, and these may lead to different approaches to a Science Of Cybersecurity.
>
> **Aristotelian science** was one of definition and classification. Perhaps it represents the earliest stage of an observational science, and it is seen here both in attempts to provide a precise characterisation of what security means but also in the taxonomies of vulnerabilities and attacks that presently plague the cyberinfrastructure.
>
> A **Newtonian science** might speak in terms of mass and forces, statics and dynamics. Models of computational cybersecurity based in automata theory and modelling access control and information might fall in this category, as well as more general theories of security properties and their composability.

A **Darwinian science** might reflect the pressures of competition, diversity, and selection. Such an orientation might draw on game theory and could model behaviours of populations of machines infected by viruses or participating in botnets, for example. A science drawing on the ideas of **prospect theory** and **behavioural economics** developed by Kahneman, Tversky, and others might be used to model risk-perception and decision-making by organizations and individuals.

As we consider Dr Landwehr's list of the different kinds of science, perhaps a salient approach to attacking this kind of problem—for a 'social' plus 'technological' science such as Cybersecurity—would be to include all of these different approaches. However one cannot run before one is able to walk—and so it may be best to produce an **Aristotelean science** first.

Ergo it would be—above all—a science that focusses on definition, classification, axioms and establishing taxonomies of threats and countermeasures—plus topic: structure/relationship 'maps' for all concepts etc.

I am in agreement with Dr Landwehr when he says that he does not believe that it is possible to develop a science of Information Security—without first establishing an **observational science** that identifies what we are dealing with in the first place (i.e. recognition of particular security-related things/events and subsequent definition of object/process classes etc). Accordingly, we become able to know what kinds of phenomena to look for, measure, model and control. However, as you shall see, elements of the other kinds of science described by Dr Landwehr are evident in our approach—and as developed in the present book.

For example, our approach is more akin to a **Newtonian science** that places emphasis on fundamental objects, processes, forces and their composability. In this respect, when evaluating my treatise, note the emphasis upon and identification of, the different kinds of foundational 'building blocks' for a science of Cybersecurity.

Now whenever we begin to speak of any aspect of data/information gathering, organisation, manipulation and/or communication etc; we are dealing with computers and related topics. Typically present are five fundamental categories (or domains) of computing operations as follows:

- **PROCESSING**—deals with aspects of data entry, gathering, movement, combination and transformation (local/remote);

- **STORAGE**—deals with aspects of data permanence and preservation (local/remote);

- **PRESENTATION**—deals with aspects of data connection, visibility and display (local/remote);

- **COMMUNICATION**—deals with aspects of data transfer between networked devices and/or computers (local/remote).

- **COMMAND AND CONTROL**—deals with aspects of the automatic, semi-automatic, plus remote control, of networked devices (systems/machines/mechanisms) and/or computers (local/remote).

Our subject shall be the formation of a comprehensive definition for the key domain of ***Communications Security***—for private, secret and/or open datum(s)—and with respect to the preservation of ***Social Accessibility Status*** *(all actors)*.

Space limitations preclude a full Cybersecurity analysis; nevertheless, aspects of the argumentation and logical integers introduced here will be applicable to all computing domains.

Foundations Of A New Science

If we are to establish a new **Science Of Cybersecurity**, then it is vitally important to be certain that we are founding—or building—upon a firm substructure. In normal scientific language, the foundation, or basis of any argument is named as the hypothesis, and is often a subject's supposition, or primary subject-matter.

Ergo, before we can attempt to discuss what Communications Security is, could or should be; and explore the nature of this particular area of computer science; we must first establish a clear idea of what is meant by the term **data/information security.**

CIA Triad

A simple security model is the CIA Triad[1]; standing for **Confidentiality**, **Integrity** and **Availability**.

In this context, **confidentiality** (equivalent to privacy) is a set of rules that limits access to information; **integrity** is maintaining the consistency, accuracy, and trustworthiness of data over its entire life cycle, and **availability** is a guarantee of reliable access to the information by authorised people.

Origins of the CIA Triad are lost in the mists of time.

However, we do see early references in the 1990s InfoSec Community to the CIA Triad.

---

[1] N.B. The CIA Triad does **not** have anything to do with the US Central Intelligence Agency!

Notably also the concepts of confidentiality, integrity and availability of information have been used by war generals for quite some time; for instance, one can see Julius Caesar operating along these lines during the Gallic Wars.

Figure-1 below shows a neat representation of the interrelated nature of the different facets of the CIA Triad.

Figure 1: CIA Triad

Whilst all three elements of the CIA Triad are crucially important in any Information Security scenario whatsoever; in truth Cybersecurity is normally understood to be concerned more with **data privacy**. In other words— Cybersecurity often deals with aspects of just two facets of the triad, **confidentiality** and **availability** (including meta-data); whilst leaving the third (data-integrity—systematic aspects) to be dealt with by broader system reliability concerns.[2]

Ergo, we are concerned here—chiefly—with aspects of the *confidentiality* and *availability* of private and secret data.

Cybersecurity Definition

Before we can begin to discuss Cybersecurity in detail, we must define our primary topic…

> **CYBERSECURITY (communications domain):** The state of being protected against criminal or unauthorised use of electronic data, or the measures taken to achieve this. Whereby all illegitimate actor(s)—the unwarranted human plus machine actor(s), and their helper(s)—are prevented from **Accessing** (ie. Finding, Contacting and Knowing/Using) a private/secret datum's **Form** and/or **Content**. Protection normally involves use of security protocols/mechanisms for **Locking**, **Blocking** and **Concealing** all relevant system access gateways (for said datum(s)).

In summary, Cybersecurity is the protection of social accessibility status for an item of meaning—or a datum— and as such refers to the protection of **secrecy**, **privacy** or **openness** of meaning; or the safe transfer/storage/access of single/multiple datum(s) between/for actors(s)/human(s).

---

[2] N.B. Data Integrity remains a vital factor/goal; only here we collapse said requirement to the datum-copy (aggregated) level; and ignore broader system reliability aspects.

Do not worry if you find the above definition of Cybersecurity complex, overly-technical and/or opaque.

In truth, we have jumped ahead of ourselves by several steps. In fact, the primary goal of this *entire* book is to provide an adequate definition of Cybersecurity; including all of its terms, concepts and principles etc. We simply offered up the above definition at this early stage, in order to give the reader a preview of where we are headed.

Without further ado, let us now begin—and with a look at the central issues of Cybersecurity Science.

Founding Premises

We shall base our Cybersecurity treatise on three founding arguments (or premises) as follows:

A) CYBERSECURITY IS AN OBSERVATIONAL PLUS DESCRIPTIVE SCIENCE: Cybersecurity is impossible to develop as a logical subject of study—without first establishing an **observational plus descriptive science** that identifies what we are dealing with in the first place. Ergo, we become able to know what kinds of phenomena to look for, measure, model and control. Accordingly, desired is a science that focusses on observation, definition, classification, axioms and establishing taxonomies of threats and countermeasures— plus topic: structure/relationship 'maps' for all relevant concepts, events, processes and objects etc.

Data Integrity Assurance: For any particular communication instance, adjudging whether or not the communicated datum(s) [i.e. meaning aspect(s) + meta-data] have been: A) Securely delivered, used by, or made available to, the desired parties (authorized ones only); plus: B) Delivered whole and intact; and: C) Aggregated together in a correct sequence—is a difficult and complex process. Normally multiple datum(s) are bundled together and communicated in a carefully ordered sequence or aggregated unit of data (i.e. as in a document); and an integrity checksum value is assigned to the data-unit, whilst this checksum is then securely communicated to the receiver to provide assurance that said data-unit (plus meta-data) is intact/whole and has not been tampered with or damaged in any way.

B) SUBJECT OF STUDY: Cybersecurity (communications domain) is defined as the protection of social accessibility status for an item of meaning—or a Datum—and as such refers to the protection of **secrecy, privacy** or **openness** of meaning; or the safe transfer/storage/access of single/multiple Datum(s) between/for human(s) [see later chapters for term definition(s)]. **Legitimate** Social Accessibility (or Privacy) Status exists in one of three distinct and non-intermediate states; named as **Open, Private** and **Secret** (for a detailed explanation of the legitimate/illegitimate types of privacy status—see discussion(s) in later sections).[3]

In accordance with the aforementioned principal statement of Cybersecurity theory; the founding principles for the entire subject matter of communications security are established as, and wholly contained within, the—**Science Of Cybersecurity Framework—or SCF**—which consists of a specific list of Axioms and associated Lexicon definitions (see book contents plus end-notes).

C) CYBERSECURITY METRICS: For a practical science—such as Cybersecurity—it is vitally important to establish appropriate and clearly defined targets. Accordingly, we recognise **continuous security** as the key goal—whereby—we establish that **Absolute Security** is a kind of ruler or metric—being one that indicates/reflects the specific (time-bound) Social Accessibility (or Privacy) Status for a nominal item/datum-copy. An item is absolutely secure when it is—at the present epoch—out of reach of any unsafe actors—and there are no illegitimate item-copies. Absolute Security is a (potentially) measurable protective status—and one that does not have to be indisputably knowable/possible/true—or permanent—in order for it to be a valid goal or metric in relation to an item/datum-copy.

---

[3] N.B. Our choice and use of the monikers Open, Secret and Private; refer to the three fundamental, mutually-exclusive and **legitimate** categories of Privacy-Status possible for a secure datum (see Chapters 2,3). These monikers may seem somewhat arbitrary; however other categories of Privacy-Status can only exist for **illegitimate** or insecure datum(s) (i.e. unprotected ones). Outside of the present treatise, other monikers may be used, referring (for example) to one (or more) of the three fundamental classes of Privacy-Status (for example in normal usage private/secret may be interchanged or used identically referring to one specific type of Privacy-Status or security protection etc).

Ergo, we have neatly moved emphasis away from somewhat nebulous and ill-defined talk of 'systems' security—and onto datum-copies—in accordance with a basic theme of the present book (communications security = social accessibility protection for datum-copies).

By so doing, seemingly we have 'collapsed' Communications Security into a domain that deals solely with with the protection of multiple datum(s) of meaning; and we ostensibly ignore the system *processing, storage, presentation* and *control* domains altogether.

However this is not so in reality; because by taking an 'informational' perspective focussed on datum(s), we assume that the other computing domains must be sufficiently well designed to maintain any and all identified security targets/methods present for the communicated datum(s) themselves (ref. communications domain).

Consequently, we shall define an **Absolute Security TARGET** [Axiom 12]—for a point-to-point communication system—as the replication of a single instance (or primary-copy) of a datum—from one socially restricted access-node to another. In other words, it is the **single-copy-send** of a datum from one party to another

Note that the other party may be the same party in another place/time; whereby no illegitimate—socially accessible—nth-party copies exist whatsoever (hopefully persistently).

Secondly, **Absolute Security METHOD(S)** [Axiom 62]—are continually working security: systems, rules, actors, networks, programs, defences and human/automatic operational procedures etc; that protect: An Absolute Security TARGET.

Hypothesis

In summary, one can state that the entire subject matter of Cybersecurity relates to a deliberate attempt to establish clear, valid, plus quantifiable actor accessibility targets—or metrics—for any Cybersecurity scenario whatsoever.

Whereby we in turn become able to know which specific features and events/processes to implement, allow, prevent and measure in a practical security system.

Accordingly, we (hopefully) learn how to install valid security systems; and in order to produce effective countermeasures for any and all known/possible Cyberthreats/vulnerabilities.

An Observational plus Descriptive Science

The definition of an—**observational science**—is a field of science where controlled observations cannot be made in order to study cause(s)-and-effect(s) (contrasted with an experimental science where localised tests are possible).

An example of a pure observational science is astronomy, where a person cannot change the movement or any aspect of the sun, moon and stars, nor can he visit them. It seems clear that Cybersecurity is (at least partially) an observational science—the same being one where observations of cause(s)-and-effect(s) may be extremely difficult—if not impossible to—identify, model, affect and/or control.

For Cybersecurity this is so due to the hugely complex—plus constantly evolving—nature of (for example) a computer connected to the open network.

Whereby not only will that same (networked) computer be (potentially) subject to countless (difficult to understand) Cyberthreats and constantly changing exploit vulnerabilities; but also we may have (multiple) human antagonists (plus their machine 'helpers') present—who try to sweep aside any security protections that happen to be in place. Ergo, Cybersecurity must be—at least to some extent—potentially—unpredictable/out-of-control.

Accordingly constant **analytical observation** of real-world security system(s); becomes a critical part of any practical Cybersecurity scenario whatsoever.

Causality

What about cause-and-effect relationships within the highly technical field of Cybersecurity?

Whilst we do not prescribe to the wholly 'unscientific' proscription—and/or 'unscientific' stereotyping—of Cybersecurity, we do recognise that Cybersecurity is at least in some senses similar to a war or political struggle. In other words our (networked) computer systems exist in a constantly changing plus highly unstable (social and technical) environment where an unknown number of (possibly unknown) enemies may at any moment launch a successful Cyber-attack.

Notable however—is that wars are **won by the application of science**!

But it seems that science alone may not be sufficient to protect us forever. Clever opponents (armed with ever-improving technical tools/methods) work constantly to try and break any security measures that are put in place.

Consequently, we must accept that Cybersecurity (if it is a science) is not governed by purely logical predictive method(s) alone—but rather requires observational/corrective methods by testing/patching threat countermeasures in the real environment in which the system is/can/will-be deployed and/or used.

It is not that cause-and-effect relationships are unimportant when it comes to Cybersecurity, or that they have become in some way redundant; but rather that causality becomes difficult to source/follow/predict and employ—and/or may be masked by complexity—or else rendered inapplicable in a deliberate fashion by the deceptive and illicit methods of an opponent.

In sum, I would suggest that we should not turn our backs on science/logic when it comes to Cybersecurity analysis/design/implementation. But rather we must make visible/cogent all of the (eminently logical) factors involved—including detailed knowledge of both real and potential threats/countermeasures; and through application/wielding of theory, perceptive and monitoring skills, classification, modelling—plus above all—by using the principles of **logical analysis**.

Description

A **descriptive science** is a category of science that involves observing, recording, describing and classifying phenomena. Descriptive research is sometimes contrasted with hypothesis-driven research, which is focused on testing a particular hypothesis by means of experimentation (i.e. probing the 'real' world for data).

Application of a descriptive science would seem to be a highly appropriate methodology for an observational subject matter, and especially for a (potentially) unpredictable science such as Cybersecurity. Whereby emphasis is placed on recognising/defining what is occurring; and/or could, can or may just possibly occur; and in terms of a totality of multi-dimensional environmental-factors/eventualities plus assessment of likely antagonists.

Overall, we do accept that Cybersecurity does possess elements that seem to be in close accordance with those features recognisable as a descriptive science.

Design and Modelling

Some experts have used the terms "descriptive sciences" and "design sciences" as an updated version of the distinction between basic—or theoretical—and applied science. Descriptive sciences are those that seek to describe reality, while design sciences seek useful knowledge for human activities.

Dr Landwehr introduced the interesting idea that Cybersecurity might be more akin to an engineering school that develops and teaches a **science of design**; whereby teachers/theory can only offer useful guidance, but no set of hard and fixed rules, to the developer of a security system. The principles of a science of design are indeed highly applicable to Cybersecurity subject matter(s)—whereby participants can benefit from the opportunity to outwit their opponents by means of the application of creative and inventive measures.

Science Of Cybersecurity Framework (SCF)

In order to establish a logically coherent statement of basic theory, and to enable orderly progression for the same; we hereby define the Science Of Cybersecurity Framework (SCF) Version 1.0. Whereby, the SCF comprises all of the various principles, axioms, concepts and term definitions contained in this book—amounting to a complete characterisation of the entire subject matter of Cybersecurity (ref. communications domain).

Summary (Cybersecurity as a Science)

In summary, and taking all factors into consideration, it does seem to be the case that—Cybersecurity is a science that may be best served/applied (fundamentally)—as a science that focusses on **observation** and **definition**; wherein the partitioner places emphasis on classification, axioms and establishing taxonomies of threats and countermeasures—plus topic: structure/relationship 'maps' for all concepts/objects and processes/events etc.

In a nutshell, we embrace the scientific method(s) of **observation**, **description** and **design**, plus adding in the 'magic' ingredient of logical cause-and-effect. Accordingly within the boundaries of logical analysis—it is possible to develop a taxonomy of all the different Cyber-threats that are possible in a nominal network security system.

Cybersecurity applications/systems can thereby retain all the trusted benefits of the observational and theoretical approaches; whilst leaving room for creative—and inventive—countermeasure solutions (see Appendix D).

Secrecy and Privacy

In the spirit of establishing thorough definition(s) for all of the words and concepts employed in any discussion related to the subject matter of Cybersecurity; we hereby provide the following terminological foundations in relation to the topic of privacy.

Private, Secret And Open Thoughts

A *secret-thought* is a thought that occurs in the mind of an individual, and has not left the 'mind' of the thinker to enter another person's mind and/or machine's 'mind' (yet). Secret-thoughts may, in fact, be related to thoughts originating in other people's minds; but vital here is that nobody else yet knows, or can easily discover the contents of the same, or that the thought has been (or is being) thought by the thinker.

Secret-thoughts are an individual's natural property alone. Others may be able to guess a secret-thought; but that is different from certain knowledge. With secret-thoughts the thinker is in (more or less) complete control over any communicated thought contents.

A secret-thought is—bound in/with time—because what was once secret, may no longer be secret at some date/epoch in the future.

Secret-thoughts are protected from discovery by others—and are hidden/concealed in some way. Secrecy is a state of being/existence for the thought itself. Secret-thoughts, by definition, exist in a single mind—or no mind—in the case of 'lost' secret-thoughts.

Every *open-thought* was once a secret-thought; but has subsequently been communicated to other mind(s), or else written down and stored in a place freely accessible to others. Open-thoughts are essentially, social thoughts.

Open-thoughts exist (potentially at least) in everyone's mind(s); and the originator may have little control over how, when, and to whom such thoughts are communicated. Both open and secret-thoughts may be singular or composite; and thus be comprised of thoughts and sub-thoughts copied from elsewhere, and link-to and/or subsume (or represent) many other thoughts/patterns.

What differentiates open from secret-thoughts is their state of discoverability—and in this respect a thought is only secret, if there can be no possibility of transfer to another mind (at a specific epoch).

Writing down a thought in a public arena, would potentially nullify secrecy (in the future); and hence such an exposed thought may no longer be classified as secret, and because it is—potentially discoverable (it is a hidden/lost open-thought until then).

It is vital to recognise that not only original-thoughts start out as secret. When someone thinks/duplicates an unusual thought originated by someone else, then the fact that they are thinking this same thought, may constitute a secret—and hence a changed thought—by itself. What matters is whether another party is able to access unique/original thought contents (or has the possibility of so doing).

Datum(s) are herein rendered analogous/bound to thoughts/ideas; and are named as the fundamental units of information and/or related informational computation.

A third class of thought is identified as a ***private-thought***; defined as a thought which has-been/will-be shared amongst a restricted group of individuals.

Private-thoughts possess a special feature, in that they are distributed to a limited number of people; and hence some form of social sharing plus protection is implied; and in order to protect the status of a private-thought, and to prevent it from morphing into an open-thought.

Discoverability is restricted and controlled by some mechanism/lock/key, plus social trust.

Total Secrecy / Privacy

It is insightful to ponder a little further on the nature (and fundamental definition(s)) of secrecy and privacy…

To begin with, let us imagine that you are standing next to someone in a private location, before passing a real-world object to that person, and in a such manner that ensures (for argument's sake) that this same action cannot be overlooked/discovered. Accordingly, it is easy to understand—that this act is absolutely private.

However things are not quite so simple—when you pass datagrams (messages, folders and files etc) across a remote wired/wireless communication system (aka the Internet). In particular, such a data-transfer may be visible and/or exposed to the actions of other programs/ actors/people—and primarily because it (the act) has a public aspect—in terms of the visibility/accessibility of associated communications data. This is because the network itself is (normally) public—or open.

For example, the packetised-data may be visible, and/or the wired/wifi/3G/4G/5G communications data may be observable/hackable; and/or the associated Internet traffic could be spied upon in some way etc.

Regardless of whether or not any exposed—or persisted—datum-copies normally exist on the communication system itself (i.e. central/cloud copies)—one has to admit—that on an open-network—aspects of the live communication process may be visible to nth-parties. Hence communications must be (theoretically) no longer entirely private/secret—or at least in terms of the existence of any transferred packets etc; and most probably in terms of other aspects of the datum-copy's form.

Ergo, we are forced to conclude—that total privacy/secrecy—in relation to the—sum total of all aspects of a datum-copy's form/content—for such a digital communication process—is quite simply, impossible to achieve. Another problem, in our terms, relates to the mixing-up—of the media of storage, transfer and access—and in way(s) that likewise result in aspects of a datum -copy's form being rendered publicly visible/accessible.

Our discussion implies that you (the owner of the copy)—plus the system designer(s)/operator(s)—must choose which aspects of the datum-copy—and hence communication process as whole—to make secret/private.

However certain aspects will, nevertheless, remain public! In other words—security is all about deciding which aspects of a datum-copy can be wholly removed from public view (aka beholder's share etc)—and which (inevitably public) aspects to protect using locking/ blocking/concealment mechanism(s) etc.

We can conclude that a secret/private communication process—taking place in a semi-public arena always has public aspects—or facets—regardless of how powerful—or impenetrable—may be the protection mechanism(s).

Secrecy Defined

WHAT is secrecy, in-and-of-itself? And how do we keep something secret? What are the fundamental techniques for attaining/securing/preserving secrecy?

Unquestionably, these are fundamental questions (for any society)—and answering the same can help us to understand secrecy at a deep, and even philosophical, level.

Ergo, we wish to come up with a strict definition for the term. In this respect, right away, we notice that it is necessary to protect an item by concealing, blocking and/or locking its specific material-form and/or inner-meaning from others. In other words we must prevent other people/systems/agents from finding, contacting, copying and/or knowing the item.

Obviously we can build a protective barrier (i.e walls) around the item (i.e place it in a safe/vault); and then create a locked door—being one that requires some form of pass-key in order to open.

Alternatively, we can prevent any unwarranted actor/person from reaching it—by means of blocked/inaccessible pathways. Finally, we could hide the item in a secret location known only to ourselves—and the same being one that is—for some reason—difficult to see/find by other people.

But all of this begs the question—what is the common feature of secrecy—and can we identify any fundamental characteristics—in terms of being able to attain it by means of a particular method?

Put simply, attaining/defending secrecy—for any item—may be defined as protecting the material/virtual-form of a thing; or restricting its contents to the actual owner of the thing alone. In other words, we wish to protect the secrecy of the item—in terms of who can see, know and/or change it.

The concept of secrecy is at the same time—and equally—socially defensive (broadest possible terms) and socially restrictive (narrowest possible terms). Above all, secrecy requires that the genuine entry-method(s)—or valid pathway(s)—used to reach the item's form/content—must be exceptionally well-defended (in social accessibility terms)—and remain so perpetually. Ergo, any and all unauthorised pathways/surreptitious entry-methods must be untenable/inaccessible for all parties (illicit actors).

Additionally—authorised entry-method(s)—must be of such a form/type/kind that they cannot be attained/guessed/stumbled-upon, or otherwise discovered/used by any unwarranted-party/breaching-technique (including statistical and brute-force methods etc). In a nutshell, secrecy is the attenuation/whittling-down—or drastic reduction—of unwarranted accessibility options (entry-methods/pathways) for an item—whereby the (relatively scarce) authentic entry-method(s)/pathway(s) are perpetually out-of-reach to any and all unwarranted people/actors.

Indeed this is what communications security is at a fundamental level, the precise definition of a protective status (privacy, secrecy) for an item (ref. Social Accessibility Status).

Absolute Security

You may sometimes here a security professional say something like: 'in the field of information security— (there are no absolutes)—except that (there are no absolutes)'—or words to that effect.

Perhaps these same people do not realise that this statement is, in actual fact, an example of circular reasoning—or a logical statement that restates the premise as the conclusion. Anyway, a few prominent security experts—have expressed objection to the word 'absolute' in the present book's terminology.

What I think these same experts are alluding to—is the impossibility of making any Absolute Security predictions; or attaining perpetual—ever-lasting—security protection in relation to information that is stored/transferred by means of networked computers.

Such an interpretation is correct—because security is (and always has been throughout history) an **arms race** between those who seek to protect information and those who seek to circumvent those protections. Today's best ciphers will doubtless be trivially broken in the future at some point. However, it seems that the dissent surrounding the word "absolute" is due to varied interpretations of what it means.

Avoiding confusion, multiplication and lack-of-rigour with respect to our term/concept definitions would seem to be an essential ingredient for any Cybersecurity Science. Ergo—by means of the present exposition, I would like to fully define "absolute" in the context of security literature— and also in relation to the present book in particular.

Need For Metrics

Let us begin by assuming that the term 'Absolute Security'—alludes to a system that is permanently impregnable for all time (i.e. it can never be broken into).

That is not what I am claiming here for the meaning of the term Absolute Security—and for several reasons. Here I shall define Cybersecurity as protection of **Privacy Status** for an item; and Absolute Security (for a private-copy) as single-copy-send—or no access whatsoever for unsafe-actors (see discussion(s) in chapters 2, 3).

Wherein Absolute Security is a kind of ruler or metric—one that indicates/reflects the specific Accessibility Status (or Privacy Status) for the datum-copy. An item is absolutely secure when it is—at the present epoch—out of reach of any unsafe actors—and there are no illegitimate copies.

Henceforth, I would suggest that Absolute Security is a measurable protective status—and one that does not have to be possible—or permanent—in order for it to be a valid goal or metric in relation to a copy.

Accordingly, as previously stated, we have neatly moved emphasis away from systems—and onto datum-copies—in accordance with the basic theme of the present theory (security = protecting datum-copies). However any copy-related insecurity must be the result of security system failure(s)—so we must ask: how/where do these problems arise?

In the present book, we take a datum-centric approach to all of the key issues of Cybersecurity; and in so doing we adopt a meaning or communication-centric perspective; in the belief that any and all attendant systematic design requirements will become apparent.

Complexity Problem

Evidently, computing systems are extremely complex, varied and changeable—and many uncertainties can be the case for a datum-copy existing in a public networked computing environment (even an ostensibly protected one). It follows that the privacy status for any item on a networked computer system—is a situation-specific property that may (quite possibly) change over time.

However this does not mean that we should adopt an attitude whereby we just shrug our shoulders whenever a leak/data-breach occurs. And then make the excuse that when it comes to security there are no absolutes—or even idealised metrics with which to judge security status.

Systematic security is therein misrepresented as (forever) a contradiction in terms—something not even worthy of comprehensive definition and/or accurate measurement.

Inevitably, security experts encourage us all to install protective mechanisms, but often without providing the concordant means to adequately adjudge/measure if they are, in fact, working. It would seem essential to first-of-all define the security goal for a private datum-copy—being Absolute Security (i.e. single-copy-send for a specific communication instance). A clear security target is required in order to have any chance of discovering whether we have attained it—or lost it—and why!

Surely we cannot be expected to just passively await the arrival of evil-tidings in the form of system exploits—without full knowledge of what is the key goal/measure of communications security (ref. private/secret datums and single-copy-send).

Unsurprisingly, such an 'no-absolutes' attitude pre-shadows a built in excuse for the designers of security systems. It gives them a get-out-clause; because they do not have to explain how or why the security targets failed—and because there are none—or at least highly specific ones like single-copy-send—complete with appropriate logical happenings.

Continuous Security

We may conclude that successful exploits are not the result of a lack of absolutes in security—that is a wholly illogical argument—and because it renders uncertainty/ lack-of-knowledge/poor-defences as a valid excuse for failure.

Whereby we put the symptom ahead of the cause. Rather we must accurately define continuous security as the goal— which is itself a type of absolute—or how else would you define successful protection of privacy—but as a kind of temporary permanence to be constantly achieved. Please note, that I am not claiming here that we cannot have zero-day-exploits—or unknown-unknowns in terms of system design/operations—but rather that we should wake up and smell the gunpowder.

We must seek to identify bone-fide explanations for our security failure(s)—and not hide behind logical-conundrums/meaningless-mantras. Rather, we embrace the truth—that it is a complete lack of precise, logical and measurable—security targets that holds us back.

N.B.—Here in this book we are (ostensibly) concerned solely with aspects of the communications domain of Cybersecurity—nevertheless—despite the fact that we often refer to the key goal of preserving **social accessibility protection**; this accessibility protection should be read as including any and all types of actor(s)/system(s); covering human and machine actor(s)—plus their helper systems, processes, mechanisms etc.

Accordingly, we hereby define (ref. communications security):

A) The **Absolute Security Method(s)** for a communications system as consideration of every aspect of security to produce an all-round system that works coherently as a whole against all types of illicit hacking/exploit attacks, using the full gamut of known defensive techniques. We do not mean that the system is permanently impregnable for all time (i.e. that it can never be broken). Absolute security is a time-bound attainable ideal (or potential state), with a robust theoretical footing to back up its practicality and achievability.

We also provide a second related definition:

B) The **Absolute Security Target** for a private datum-copy is defined as single-copy-send—whereby it is the communications system's Absolute Security method(s) that helps to deliver the same.

Note that both definitions are ideal system status metrics to be achieved and not permanent features that somehow self-perpetuate.

Need For Absolutes

In conclusion, we need absolutes—and the concept of Absolute Security—not because it is a nieve dream-like state of system/data safety. We need the target(s) and method(s) of Absolute Security because these are idealised goal(s)—or assurance objective(s)—and reflect the very status values that we seek to measure our success and/or failure against.

We could choose another grouping of words to represent the goal of continuous security (i.e comprehensive security). Nevertheless the underlying security metric is the same—a system that strives towards ideal and (hopefully) attainable security protection for our private information.

Synopsis

The arguments developed in the present book chart close-to-the-wind in terms of exploring relationships between a host of technical and human-centric concepts/principles (hopefully to useful effect).

Overall, we seek to unify the technical and human—opportunities and risks—for information security.

As stated—communications security is protection of privacy of meaning. However the simple logical clarity of this statement changes in certain subtle and difficult to determine ways—when it crosses-over into the realm of cyber. In particular—in the digital-world—nothing is entirely private—and one must lock/block/conceal all illicit entry-methods for secret/private items. As many as possible of the physical, virtual and meaning gateways must be protected—and in order to retain any chance of achieving Absolute Security (see later discussions).

In summary, one can state that the entire subject matter of Cybersecurity, relates to a deliberate attempt to establish clear, valid, plus quantifiable social accessibility targets—or metrics—for any Cybersecurity scenario whatsoever.

Whereby we in turn become able to know which specific features and events/processes to implement, allow, prevent and measure in a practical security system. Accordingly, we learn how to install valid security systems; and in order to produce effective countermeasures for any and all known/possible Cyberthreats (see Appendix C).

In the end-notes you will find a complete Lexicon of Cybersecurity terms, plus a listing of the introduced Axioms upon which the present treatise is built.

Over coming sections we shall explore Cybersecurity theory with sufficient rigour, depth, breadth plus integration; such that a new all encompassing picture—and detailed philosophy—of the entire field is formed. Overall it is our contention that the resulting holistic point of view—amounts to nothing less than the beginning of an actual Science Of Cybersecurity.

We leave it to the reader to judge the extent to which we have achieved our aim.

* * * * *

Infographics

IN THIS BOOK we develop a number of different kinds of **InfoGraphics** that relate to the field of Cybersecurity (communications domain); and it is our hope that you will find these diagrams useful, and especially in terms of understanding the logical SCF theory.

In accordance with the basic principles and theory of InfoGraphics; in producing our Cybersecurity diagrams, we have attempted to abide by efficient and effective graphical design principles and visual design best practice.

It is also our belief that any useful InfoGraphic should tell a story, in and of-itself; plus it should reward close attention/study. Above all we wanted our InfoGraphics to afford principles of logical analysis; that is to aid in the process whereby an onlooker wishes to explore the origins of HOW and WHY things come to be as they are within the Cybersecurity field as a whole, plus to see relations and explanations on all scales.

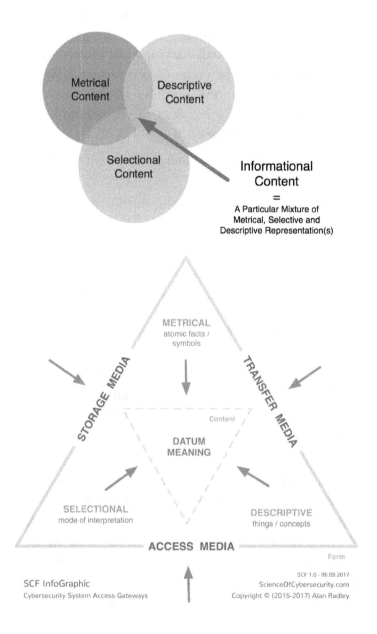

Figure 2 (A & B): Informational Content & Datum Meaning

CHAPTER 2

Communications Security

(Treatise Foundation)

THE SUBJECT at hand is the secure transfer of meaning between individual human beings—using networked computers. Our goal is to characterise a point-to-point communication system for replicating *information patterns*—encapsulated as discrete units of data *(e.g. messages/files/folders)*—between remote computer nodes; whilst protecting the social integrity (privacy) of said patterns in place and time. A second goal of this book is to establish a safe procedure for point-to-point information transfer—and by means of logically consistent definitions, axioms, analysis and exposition.

The British physicist Professor Donald MacKay (1922-1987) once said that the informational content of a message/representation consists of three components; **metrical, selectional**, and **descriptive** [1]. Accordingly, in terms of the point-to-point transfer of information units (datums) between two humans—or the one-to-one replication of meaning from a sender to receiver—we can differentiate between the information pattern that is sent (i.e the atomic, symbolic and/or *metrical* data being replicated—the digital 0s and 1s etc), and the *selectional* and *descriptive* capacity of the receiving system/human.

In other words, the receiver engages in a process of interpretation by utilising his or her *'beholder's share'* [2].

Hence the meaning of a message is crucially dependent on the specific way(s) in which the receiver decodes and interprets the message. Ergo meaningful, effective and efficient communication between two parties depends upon a certain degree of synchronisation and agreement in terms of factors such as *language, experience, truth, history,* plus *mode* and *context* of the communication process itself.

Whereby it is important to realise that the entire subject matter of (communications) **Cybersecurity** depends upon—and is (entirely) developed from—the axiomatic statements and principles presented in the previous three paragraphs.

In sum, this book is a characterisation of said axioms.

We begin with a simple question—*what is security*—in-and-of-itself—and especially in terms of digital information sharing? In order to be able to formulate an answer we must narrow our field of study—and concern ourselves solely with person-to-person (point-to-point) information transfer. We can differentiate this topic from all other information transfer types which involve either a source-point and/or end-point that is not a human being.

Ignored methods include *machine-to-machine, machine-to-person,* and *person-to-machine* techniques.

In other words; we are not concerned with those cases where a computer *initiates* transfer(s) of information between machines, or does so automatically from machine to human or vice-versa.[4]

---

[4] N.B. Most principles—discussed herein—for private/secure point-to-point information transfer—apply also to these other communication types.

Communication Of Meaning

A **datum** of any idea or thing is a *pattern of meaning*, an abbreviated description, definition or set of 'facts' concerning the thing in question; typically prescribing an event, object, feeling, etc.; in token of, as a sign, symbol, or evidence of something [Axiom 1].

Datums are typically expressed within the boundaries of a specific language, medium, media and/or code; and normally each datum has an inherent lifetime whereby it may be created, stored, communicated, replicated, lost and/or destroyed etc. Each datum has a human and/or machine *creator/author,* plus normally human *owner(s)* and *user(s)* (ref. social accessibility (or privacy) status) [Axiom 2].

Datums come in three kinds [Axiom 3]:

- A **private datum** is accessible only by a restricted group of people—or a particular set of human beings; and is inaccessible to all other persons [Axiom 3.1].

- A **secret datum** is accessible only by a single human being—typically the owner and often the author; and is inaccessible to all other persons [Axiom 3.2].

- An **open datum** is (potentially) accessible by anyone— or by an unrestricted group of people [Axiom 3.3].

A **communication system** is a system or facility for transferring datum(s)/patterns-of-meaning between persons and equipment. The system usually consists of a collection of *individual communication networks, transmission systems, relay stations, tributary stations and terminal equipment* capable of interconnection and interoperation so as to form an integrated whole [Axiom 4].

Prior to the widespread adoption of the Internet—information assurance concerned reliable data storage/processing. But today, whilst data backups and storage etc are vital, security is more often associated with *data communications security*—herein our primary concern.

Accordingly, in the present book we shall explore just one of fifteen possible security sub-system types (communication of **private-datums**): wherein we analyse transfer of private datum-copies existing on a point-to-point communication system (whilst superficially considering aspects of data storage and presentation wherever necessary). Other sub-system security measures may be necessary in a real system—and in order to protect (for example) standard computer *processing*, *storage* and *presentation* operations; and not only for private datums but for **secret** and **open datums** as well (see Appendix A).

Throughout our exposition, we place emphasis on human-to-human communication(s)—noting: A) that whilst we recognise that interpersonal communications by means of networked computers inevitably relies on a combination of several *human-to-machine* and *machine-to-machine* communications etc; these aspects relate largely to low-level system-implementation details—and in any case said aspects fall 'down-stream' in logical and data-processing terms—and therefore any top-level security principles will normally apply throughout all low-level subsystems; and: B) that any full consideration would include aspects of all fifteen security sub-system types and would likely see the present book growing to over one thousand pages in length (see Appendix A).

We ostensibly exclude from our discussion all systems of public information sharing (i.e. *open-datums*) and social networks whereby the information transfer is *one-to-many*, *many-to-one* or *many-to-many* (i.e. Facebook/Twitter).

Accordingly—**SECURITY**—for a person-to-person communication system—can be defined as *protection* of *secrecy, privacy* or *openness of meaning*; or the safe transfer of single/multiple datum(s) between human(s) [Axiom 5].

In this context—**PRIVACY**—implies that:

- A communication system exists that connects humans together via **socially restricted access-nodes**;

- The source datum (+ meta-data) is sent from sender to receiver node as a single or **uniquely accessible copy;**[5]

- Both **access-nodes** may serve as **memory-nodes** for the datum, so long as socially unique access is preserved;

- The datum is protected from unwarranted social access *(i.e. who can see, know & change it)* by the system;

- Protection of datum access is for specified place(s) and time(s) and to achieve a state of persisted privacy.

We submit that the aforementioned list of axiomatic predicates—for secure and private communication—are valid, sound, consistent, self-evident and complete. QED.

---

[5] In this context—'uniquely accessible' refers to protection of Social Accessibility Status (or Privacy Status (i.e secret, private, or open status)) for the communicated datum; whereby (within the boundaries of) the communication system—no change(s) to the pre-existing privacy status can happen (it is immutable in terms of accessibility).

It is salient (for upcoming discussion(s)) to consider how we obtain access to any item in the real-world.

To access an item, we:

A. *Look for the item*—or scan a scene—and in order to identify/delineate the desired thing and so to discover its whereabouts, form and/or precise location (whilst distinguishing it from background clutter). Next we:

B. *Move towards the item*—or a navigate a path to its location—before grasping/touching it (whilst avoiding any path-blocking objects and/or overcoming any movement difficulties present); and finally we:

C. *Study/map/open-up/decode the item*—and in order to understand its contents and/or meaning (may require prior knowledge/special techniques and/or unlocking methods and/or unique key(s)).

In a similar fashion, we can define—**INFORMATION SECURITY**—sometimes shortened to **InfoSec**, as the practice of *defending information (datums) from unauthorised access*—including unapproved: *inspection, use, copy, disclosure, disruption, modification, recording or destruction* of said item(s).

Cybersecurity is a general term that can be used regardless of the form the data may take (e.g. electronic, physical).

Cybersecurity is the (continuous) state of preventing unauthorised communication-system actors/intruder(s) from: A) *Locating the item*; and/or B) *Grasping the item*; and/or C) *Opening-up the item*. Accordingly, we now define a process of secure information transfer—that consists of private data shared during a one-to-one information replication.

Our exposition defines (for the first time) a comprehensive set of Cybersecurity—definitions—and axiomatic first principles.

Let us now establish some logical truths.

Firstly, in summary, we can state that—**SECURITY**—for a private, secret and/or open datum is the preservation of *social accessibility status (or privacy status)*—by means of the explicit protection of said datum's status.

Protection implies the use of systems and procedures—both *human* and/or *machine*—to defend said privacy status.

Social Accessibility (Privacy) Status

The ability of a person to *see*, *know* and/or *change* a datum's form and/or content [Axiom 6].

Privacy [cp. Secrecy = datum is accessible by only one person]

A **private-thought/datum** is distributed/available to a limited number of people; and hence some form of *social sharing (& trust)*, plus *protection* is implied; and in order to prevent it from morphing into an open-thought/datum (or <u>partially</u> open-thought/datum).

Protect = Lock, Block or Conceal an item [Axiom 7].

Lock—unsafe-actor(s) cannot **open/know** an item's form/content.

Block—unsafe-actor(s) cannot **reach/grasp** an item's form/content.

Conceal—unsafe-actor(s) cannot **see/find** an item's form/content.

Security = Protect accessibility status of item.

Access = Find, contact and/or know an item.

Posses = Find (see/locate) plus contact (reach/grasp/hold) an item.

Note that within the concept/remit of locking an item; ofttimes there is a difference between *having* and *knowing* an item. Locking creates a gap/barrier or unbridgeable chasm—between possession and full access/understanding—for unauthorised parties—and especially in relation to the inner meaning of information.

Now that we have established the fundamental theory of secure communication of meaning; we need to specify the basic features of a practical security system.

We begin by identifying a **secret-datum** (analogous to a *secret-thought*)—which has not yet left the source-point (or sender's mind); and which is assumed to be unique in that nobody else can know (or discover) the precise **form** or **content** of the datum at the source-point. Once the datum arrives at the destination-point; then it is a **private-datum**; because it now exists—ostensibly solely—as an identical copy in both locations simultaneously (it is a *private-thought*).

As an aside, an **open-datum** is one that anyone may access—but *open-thoughts/datums* are not a subject of this book (see the companion book '*Self as Computer*' [3]).

Note also that the terms *private*, *secret* and *open thought*, are simply analogues of the relevant datum types (See Appendix A).

Henceforth adjudging that a point-to-point communication is private and secure; is equivalent to saying that the original unit of meaning existing at the 'source' node has, as a result of the one-to-one replication, only one accessible copy—at the 'receiver' node.

Furthermore this copy is—unequivocally—accessible only by the (trusted) human for whom the communication was intended (i.e. it is access-controlled).

We call such a process *single-copy-send—or socially secure communication* [Axiom 8]—whereby the process of communication may itself be private (no public meta-data exists); and there is no possibility of any nth-party obtaining a copy of the communicated datum.

A party might be able to guess the informational contents of the datum—or presuppose that the sender/receiver parties possess it and/or have exchanged it—but that is altogether different from certain knowledge.

Note that for a secret-datum socially secure communication restricts access to just one person. Hence the sender and receiver/viewer are the same person; and the system simply 'memorises' the datum.

In a like manner, open-datums are memorised by the system; but are then somehow made available to any party; which assumes that the system itself has a special kind of security (social accessibility protection) whereby said datum(s) are broadcast by means of the system to many/all humans. Implied here is that the system must be open-access or ubiquitous in terms of meaning dissemination.

It seems prudent—at this point—to ask another straight-forward question; specifically:

What is the nature—and architecture—of secure and private cyber-communication?

In actual fact—answering this pivotal question—will be the primary task of this short book.

And in order to formulate an answer; it is necessary to first establish the key facets of the desired communication 'chain' between the parties who wish to exchange information in a secure fashion.

Human Communication

Transfer of discrete package(s) of meaning—messages—between people; or the one-to-one replication of datum(s) between minds, plus nominal meta-data (perhaps).

Socially Secure Communication

Communication that protects socially restricted access (secrecy or privacy) for the replicated meaning—datum(s) + nominal meta-data (perhaps).

Open Communication

Communication that protects socially open access for the replicated meaning—datum(s)—and also any meta-data for the communication process itself (perhaps).

Single-Copy-Send

Communication of a datum (+ meta-data) with guaranteed social security.

Addendum: Note that accurate determination of the (measured/judged + time-bound) social accessibility status (i.e. **Privacy Status**)—and its associated protection status or **Security Status** (for a datum-copy)—means judging whether (or not) an (ostensibly) private-datum is/has-been/can-be (i.e. at-present/in-the-past/future) communicated with absolute or partial/absent security—and this may sometimes be difficult to achieve with any degree of confidence/assurance. Privacy Status (for a datum-copy) is the legitimate (but potentially transitory/changeable) social accessibility status (i.e secret, private, or open). Whereas Security Status (for a datum-copy) is a protected or unprotected Privacy Status, and accordingly may be known or unknown at any specific epoch—and is equivalent to the measured/judged privacy protection status. A datum-copy's **Privacy Status** works together with its **Security Status** to perpetuate and defend the datum's inner meaning.

Accordingly, we are now in a position to characterise Information Security (or Cybersecurity/InfoSec) in terms of an interesting new *copy-centric metric* which is defined by a few simple questions:

- How many copies are there?
- Where are the copies?
- Are the copies intact (including meta-data)?
- Who can see, know and/or change a copy?
- How long do copies hang around?

★ ★ ★ ★ ★

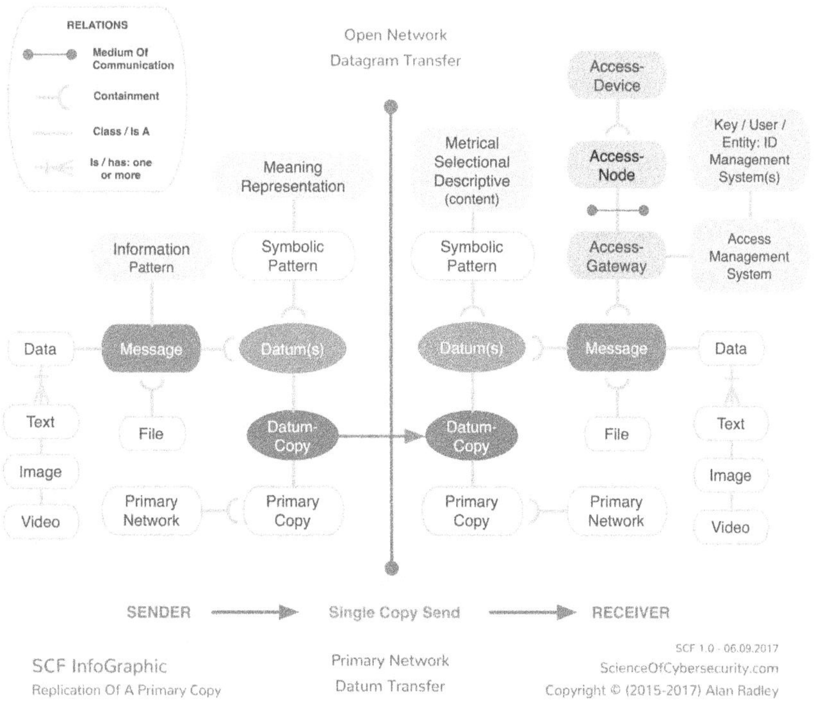

Figure 3: Replication of a Primary Copy

Primary Copy

A **primary-copy** is a place-holder for a private datum of meaning—existing within the boundaries of a point-to-point communication system; whose content and form are restricted in terms of **social access** (i.e who can see, know & change the same); whereby the datum is (ideally) communicated via *single-copy-send* from the source-point to any (and all) designated receiver-point(s) [Axiom 9].

Secondary Copy

A **secondary-copy** is a (communicated/backup) replication of a *primary-copy*—existing within (or outside) the boundaries of a point-to-point communication system—that may be **legitimately** produced by the communication process itself (e.g. a central server copy); and/or be **illegitimately** created as a result of the unwarranted activities of a hacker [Axiom 10].

N.B. Legitimate secondary copies are compatible with single-copy-send because—for example—a central-server network creates (ostensibly private) secondary copies to facilitate off-line data sharing/storage.

Christian Rogan pointed out to me that the peer-to-peer primary communication copy is also (from one perspective) the true version/copy, which leads to another solution often described as Self-Aware, whereby the object (file or data) enforces its own security protocols/policies.

Tertiary Copy

A **tertiary-copy** is a replication of a primary or secondary copy—which is generated post-communication by extracting datum(s) from a large body of communication data (e.g. a transatlantic data pipe) [Axiom 11].

N.B. Tertiary copies (whilst nefarious) are compatible with socially secure communication or single-copy-send—because for example—the datum-copies may be protected from unsafe-actors by means of strong encryption and/or coding etc.

Cybersecurity as a Science

Our ambitious aim is to establish the first founding principles/laws of a new **Science of Cybersecurity.**[6]

However some experts are adamant that Cybersecurity can never be established as a science. This is claimed to be so because—any and all social accessibility protections which are put in place will always have human opponents. That is, in this field alone, human antagonists exist—who work constantly to try and break any security measures present.

Accordingly, Cybersecurity cannot ever be a science—but is more akin to a *game, war* or *political struggle.*[7]

However, whilst the author acknowledges the existence of vital social elements within the boundaries of the highly technical field of Cybersecurity; it is his belief that application of the scientific method—consisting of a combination of *empirical observation* and *logical reasoning*—must always play a significant and foundational role in any Cybersecurity scenario whatsoever. QED.

Our goal is to bring formalism to a field that doesn't even have one—that is to bring unity, consistency and order—to the field of Information Security (communicative-aspects).

Strangely absent is any kind of top-level theory, and missing are fundamental definitions and/or first-principles etc. Ergo, the system-designer's job becomes one of—collecting **partial formalism(s)**—before somehow stitching them together. The net result is—**partial truth(s)** and/or sub-optimal approaches—or at least major difficulties.

Conversely, we seek to establish a **foundational framework** for the entire field of: information-security; and by means of comprehensive, integrated and holistic perspective(s)— combined with use of the scientific method.

---

[6] See Chapter 1: Introduction ("What kind of a science is Cybersecurity?").

[7] N.B. Wars are won by use/application of Science!

Notes

1. MacKay, Donald., Information, Mechanism and Meaning, The MIT Press, 1969.
2. Gombrich, Ernst., Art and Illusion, 1960.
3. Radley, A., Self As Computer, 2015 (later titled: World Brain).
4. Radley, A., Computer As Self, Proceedings of the 4th International Conference in Human-Computer Interaction, Tourism and Cultural Heritage, Rome, Italy., 2013.

The only truly secure system is one that is powered off, cast in a block of concrete and sealed in a lead-lined room with armed guards.
— Gene Spafford

If you think technology can solve your security problems, then you don't understand the problems and you don't understand the technology.
— Bruce Schneier

Hacker

In the computer security context, a **hacker** is someone who seeks and exploits weaknesses in a computer system or computer network. Hackers may be motivated by a multitude of reasons, such as profit, protest, challenge, enjoyment, or to evaluate those weaknesses to assist in removing them.

Logic bombs—Logic bombs are programs or snippets of code that execute when a certain predefined event occurs. Logic bombs may also be set to go off on a certain date or when a specified set of circumstances occurs.

CHAPTER 3

Why Security Is All About Copies

IN THIS THIRD chapter we overview methods for achieving privacy in terms of our interpersonal communication(s). Building on the security definitions established in the second chapter; we hereby characterise privacy as being concerned primarily with **exposed-copies** of the communicated datum (+ meta-data). Therefore Cybersecurity vulnerabilities may be mitigated by social restriction—and protection—of such copies.[8]

A second goal of this chapter is to list and classify, plus compare and contrast, the different kinds of *threats, potential exploits* and *attack-vectors/surfaces/windows* that may exist for a digital point-to-point communication system.

In simple terms we can characterise private communication as being concerned primarily with protection of ownership right(s) for **datum-copies**—or management of safe: *storage, transfer* and *social-access* for replicated datum(s) (+ meta-data).

---

[8] How many copies are there? Where are the copies? Are the copies intact (including meta-data)? Who can see, know and/or change a copy, and how long do copies hang around?

Once we recognise that any potential copy has to be either—a **primary, secondary** or **tertiary** one—then we can develop a formula for what we might term Absolute Security.

Absolute security—for a point-to-point communication instance—is the replication of a single instance (or *primary-copy*) of a private-datum from one socially restricted access-node to another [Axiom 12] [ref. Absolute Security: TARGET][9]. In other words, it is the *single-copy-send* of a datum from one party to another; whereby no—socially accessible—nth-party copies exist whatsoever (hopefully persistently—or on a long-term basis).

Likewise we can define **partial/absent security** as the existence of any unprotected—or nth-party accessible— *primary/secondary/tertiary datum-copies* [Axiom 13].

Both of these metrics—absolute and partial/absent security—are mutually-exclusive true/false values for any act of communication. It is obvious that just because a *datum-copy* has (apparently) been communicated with Absolute Security at one epoch; then that does not mean that such a status will necessarily be permanent.

Digital Media

Digital-media are electronic media used to store, transmit and receive digitised information; and may refer to any media that has been encoded in a machine-readable format. Digital-media—or simply **media**—can be created, viewed, distributed, modified and preserved on computers.

For our purposes we have compartmentalised media into three types: **storage, transfer** and **access** [Axiom 14].

---

[9] See Chapter 1: Definition of Absolute in the Context of Security.

Form and Content

A **datum** is a discrete pattern of meaning that may be transferred between minds (network access-nodes).

A **datum-copy** is a particular instantiation of a datum's pattern—that exists inside or (potentially) outside of a point-to-point communication system.

A copy has two primary aspects: firstly _form_ (the encapsulating format)—or _media of storage, communication/ delivery_, and _access_; and secondly _content_ (a representation with _metrical, descriptive_ and _selectional_ aspects) **[Axiom 15]**.

Creation of a _datum-copy_ involves instantiation of form in place and time (i.e. illustration of content in the _real_ and/or _virtual worlds_—and ultimately in a _human mind_). A _datum-copy_ has a natural **owner**—often the sender/creator of the datum **[Axiom 16]**. Ownership rights include protection of social access (e.g. secrecy, privacy, openness) for the copy—in terms of who can _see, know_ and/or _change_ the content and/or form of the copy _(ref. new owner(s)/user(s))_ **[Axiom 17]**.

When we speak of—a _datum-copy_ being **hacked** and/or a **data-breach/system-exploit** occurring—that is defined as unwarranted social access to the informational content of the datum (i.e. loss/change of privacy status) **[Axiom 18]**.

It may be that loss of privacy—extends also to aspects of the copy's form, but for the datum itself loss of privacy relates to—and consists of—purely informational content.

The OED (2nd Edition)—lists for Copy: 1) A transcript or reproduction of an original. 2) A writing transcribed from, and reproducing the contents of, another; a transcript. 3) Something made or formed, or regarded as made or formed, in imitation of something else; a reproduction, image, or imitation (e.g. electronic, physical).

Reviews of "Absolute Security"
(previous edition/name of this book)

Excellent read! Succinct and accurate on a subject that normally wanders into tangential discussions confusing and diffusing the goal. Radley breaks down today's hottest topic in a way that provides reference to students as well as guidance to the more learned. Absolute Security will give you an optimistic understanding that, even in an ever-increasing world of digital surveillance and criminal threats, ... *Absolute Security* is eminently achievable...

I found it spot on and a fine addition to the body of work on cyber-security but specifically to the discussion of privacy within communications... I see this short book as a reference document for students studying cyber security as well as an excellent read for CTOs, CSOs, CISOs, and CEOs laboring over how to analyze their needs for increased security. Absolute Security allows you to hit the highlights or dive deeper into the subject with your many charts, diagrams, and glossary of terms. Well done.

Vic Hyder - Chief Strategy Officer at Silent Circle.

Commander, U.S. Navy (SEAL), retired.

"Absolute Security" will no doubt be recognized as one of the seminal works on security, establishing definitions and clarity where others have dealt with assumptions. It is not very often that one is exposed to a work that is truly ground breaking in a field, but "Absolute Security" is one of those works. Rather than expounding on the implementation of security as many do, Dr. Alan Radley astutely asks (and then suggests an answer for) the rather naive, yet deceptively complex question "What is security?", or more precisely "How does one characterize a communication system that provides secure (private) data transfer?"

Michael Lester - **MSEE, MBA, CIPP/US, CISM.,**

Chief Information Security-Officer/Vice-President, Magenic.

All kinds of hardware/software, networking and social influencing factors can affect the privacy status of a primary, secondary and/or tertiary copy.

Potential vulnerabilities include exposed: *user IDs, logins, passwords, and private encryption keys, meta-data etc;* and each may contribute to privacy breaches.

We are now in a position to classify the different ways in which a hacker could potentially gain unwarranted access to a primary, secondary or tertiary copy of a **private-datum**.

Obviously, in order to improve the security of any communication system; one seeks to reduce the number of—**attack-surfaces/windows**—and related **attack-vectors** (for datum-copies)—and so to minimise the opportunities for break-ins to an (ostensibly) secure network.

Accordingly, we now define the principal ways in which a nominal—or generalised—communication system may be compromised; and hence result in a data-breach.

At least eight kinds of hacking/spying/eaves-dropping methods are possible; as detailed below in the list of networked system hacking methods.

———

Absolute Security Target / Methods

The **Absolute Security: TARGET**—for a point-to-point communication system—is the replication of a single instance (or *primary-copy*) of a datum—from one socially restricted access-node to another. In other words, it is the *single-copy-send* of a datum from one party to another; whereby no—socially accessible—nth-party copies exist whatsoever (hopefully persistently).

Absolute Security: METHODS—are continually working security: systems, rules, actors, networks, programs, defences and human/automatic operational procedures etc; that protect: an Absolute Security TARGET.

Networked System Hacking Methods

[See WWW.SCIENCEOFCYBERSECURITY.COM for: countermeasures]

- Cloud provider legal request—'back-door'
  —primary/secondary copy

- Transmission provider legal request
  —primary/secondary copy

- Transmission line reconstruction (remote)
  —tertiary copies

- Communications hacking (local and remote)
  —primary/secondary copy (+ tertiary copies?)

- Communications eavesdropping (environment)
  —primary/secondary copy (+ tertiary copies?)

- Cloud account hacking—'front-door'
  —primary/secondary copy

- Physical device hacking
  —primary/secondary copy

- Physical device data replication
  —primary/secondary copy

Obviously, depending upon the nature of a particular breaching technique, different impacts arise—on the primary, secondary and/or tertiary copies—as to whether or not a system is vulnerable at any particular place/time. Dependent variables include: *degree of access of the attacker to local resources, relationships of attacker to/with 'nth' parties, motivations/capabilities of attacker, attack/defence techniques, system and network vulnerabilities, and the capabilities/legal operating frameworks—plus assumptions—of all the parties involved.*

Note that for the purposes of our analysis, we make no distinctions (legal, ethical or otherwise) between an ordinary attacker; and one who may possess any supposed: *legal, moral, and/or ethical right(s)*; in relation to gaining unauthorised access to a *private-datum* (see Chapter 11).

Finally, and given what's been said; I do find myself wondering how—or even if—it is possible to mount an effective defence—permanently—against any and all cyber-attacks and unwarranted access methods.[10]

* * * * *

Access (General) = Find, Contact and/or Know an Item.

Find—actor can **see/locate** an item's form/content (cf conceal).

Contact—actor can **reach/grasp** an item's form/content (cf block).

Know—actor can **understand/open** an item's form/content (cf lock).

---

[10] In the OED (2nd Edition); **private** and/or **privacy** is defined thusly:

1) In general, the opposite of public. 2) To keep private; to seclude. 3) The state or condition of being withdrawn from the society of others, or from public interest; seclusion. 4) The state or condition of being alone, undisturbed, or free from public attention, as a matter of choice or right; freedom from interference or intrusion. Also: 5) Private or retired places; private apartments; places of retreat.

Passwords are like underwear: you don't let people see it, you should change it very often, and you shouldn't share it with strangers.
— Chris Pirillo

Hardware is easy to protect: lock it in a room, chain it to a desk, or buy a spare. Information poses more of a problem. It can exist in more than one place; be transported halfway across the planet in seconds; and be stolen without your knowledge.
— Bruce Schneier

Of course, all this good practice goes right out the window as soon as a trusted insider (like Snowden) goes rogue or is compromised. Two or even three factor authentication—something you **know** (password), something you **have** (MAC address, private Key) and/or something you **are** (finger-prints, retina scan etc)—can also greatly slow-down or prevent unauthorised access. — Radley

The mantra of any good security engineer is: **'Security is a not a product, but a process.'**
It's more than designing strong cryptography into a system; it's designing the entire system such that all security measures, including cryptography, work together.
— Bruce Schneier

CHAPTER 4

Aetiology Of A Secure Network

THE SUBJECT AT hand is network design for secure transfer of meaning between individual human beings.

Our goal is to characterise a computer network for replicating datum(s)—safely—between remote computer nodes; whilst protecting the social integrity (privacy) of said datum(s) in place and time.

A second goal of this chapter is to introduce the two basic kinds of computer network; and to identify key principles of secure network design; and by means of logically consistent performance metrics.[11]

We begin by considering security for a *primary-copy*; whereby a *private-datum* is made available on a local **access-node** within the p*rimary-network*—and by means of an **access-device** (i.e. a personal-computer) connected to the Internet (i.e. an open–network).

---

[11] Remember that earlier, we had defined **security** as **protection of privacy, openness or secrecy of meaning**—for a datum-copy. The Oxford English Dictionary—or OED (2nd Edition)—offers up the following entries for **security**: 1) the condition of being secure; 2) The condition of being protected from or not exposed to danger; safety. And also: 3) Freedom from doubt; confidence, assurance. Now chiefly, well-founded confidence, certainty.

Previously, for an act of private communication, we had assumed that a local access-node provided socially restricted access to primary-copies. However such a statement is predicated on the fact that each access-device affords an **actor-coherent** defence against any data-breaches—<u>successfully</u> [Axiom 19].

Unfortunately this may be a rather big (i.e. false) assumption; because access-device security depends upon a mishmash collection of protective methods provided by network administrators, software vendors, operating system and device manufacturers etc.

Use of the term 'network'—is problematic to say the least. This is because an access-device may be open to the data-processing activities of (any number of) inter-relating **local-actors** plus **network-actors** (i.e. human/automated ones etc). Ergo **hybrid-actors** are formed that may be partially/fully invisible, overly complex, and/or unknowable in some way—and which may be—as yet—only potentially present [Axiom 20].

————

Computer Virus

A computer virus is a program that, when executed, replicates by inserting copies of itself (possibly modified) into other computer programs, data files, or the boot sector of the hard drive. Viruses often perform some type of harmful activity on infected hosts, such as stealing hard disc space or CPU time, accessing private information, corrupting data, displaying political or humorous messages on the user's screen, spamming their contacts etc. A virus conceals the fact of its execution from a user. This is what distinguishes a virus from a trojan—a user is unaware of running a virus.

Computer Network

A **computer network** is a telecommunications network which allows computers to exchange data. On computer networks, networked computing devices exchange data with each other along network links. The connections between nodes are established using either cable or wireless media.

Datum Content Immutability

A **datum's content** may have a purely *informational meaning (be descriptive)* and/or a purely *logical meaning (be functional)*—or posses a combination of both kinds of meaning—according to context of use. However, the process of point-to-point transfer of a datum; is (normally) defined to be a transfer of information alone—and the *datum (content) is immutable* [Axiom 21].

Copy Form Mutability

Replication of a **primary-copy** (datum from + content) is transfer to a destination-point. It may be that a *copy's form (encapsulating media of storage, communication/delivery, and access etc)* changes during replication—hence *(datum) copies are mutable (form aspects)* [Axiom 22].

Security / Privacy Status

A datum-copy's **Security Status**—or protected social accessibility status—specifically its absolute or partial/absent security value—may be either: A) determined/known; or else: B) undetermined/unknown at a particular epoch. A datum-copy's **Privacy Status** (i.e secret/private/open accessibility status); works together with its Security Status (access protection) to perpetuate and defend the datum's inner meaning.

Lock, Block and/or Conceal

[i.e. Prevent an actor: knowing, contacting or finding an item]

There are basically three ways to defend/protect an item in the real-world. For example, when protecting an entrance to a house (i.e. walled safe)—we can:

A. **Lock the entrance and armour reinforce it**—or make it difficult to open/know;

B. **Block the entrance pathway**—by preventing an attacker from reaching it—for example by placing objects in the entrance-way—or by eliminating it altogether;

C. **Conceal the entrance**—and make it difficult to see/find.

Similarly for datum-copies/attack-surfaces—we can protect these in analogous way(s) [Axiom 23].

––––––

Backdoor

A so-called *backdoor* refers to either: 1) A tool installed after a compromise to give an attacker party easier access to the compromised system around any security mechanisms; or 2) A secret entry method into a system (developed by a system manufacturer/owner) which gives access by nth-parties (typically the police) to private-datums (unbeknown to the owner of said private-datums).

One-Time-Pad

In this encryption technique, a plaintext is paired with a random secret key (also referred to as *a one-time pad*). Then, each bit or character of the plaintext is encrypted by combining it with the corresponding bit or character from the pad using modular addition. If the key is truly random, is at least as long as the plaintext, is never reused in whole or in part, and is kept completely secret, then the resulting cipher-text will be impossible to decrypt or break. However, practical problems have (often) prevented one-time pads from being widely used.

Network Types

From the perspective of a digital communication system—named a **primary-network**—we can identify two basic network sub-types as follows:

> Firstly we have **cloud-server networks**; such as email, Dropbox, Facebook, Twitter etc; in which all of the communicated data is relayed by—and stored on—centralised storage facilities.

> Secondly we have **Peer-to-Peer (P2P) networks;** such as Napster, BitCoin, BitTorrent etc; the same forming a distributed network of peer-to-peer nodes that render the communicated information directly available to network participants—without the need for centralised co-ordination or central storage (but packet routing servers may still be required).

> A key advantage of P2P is that:

> *Participating users establish a virtual network, entirely independent from the physical network, without having to obey any administrative authorities or restrictions.*

Whilst it is not my intention to unduly simplify the inherent (and mammoth) complexity of computer networking as a topic, or else to disregard the great diversity of hybrid network types that are possible; space limitations preclude any further analysis of network system design in terms of implementation details.

———

Biometrics

Biometrics use physical characteristics of the users to determine access (e.g. fingerprint and/or retina scanners).

We can identify two—enforced—**coherency predicates** for Absolute Security; namely: *actor-unity* (of purpose); and *actor-integrity* (of action); for safe hardware/software operations on each access-device **[Axiom 24]**.

Similarly, *unsafe-actor* repellent/containment techniques can be used to preserve the legitimacy of data-processing operation(s) on the primary-network **[Axiom 25]**.

Moving on to consider security for the **primary-network** —plus any **secondary-network(s)**—or privileged-access networks intimately connected to the same—we are concerned here with secondary-copy protection. Accordingly, for those situations that require Absolute Security; it would seem to be good practice (at least in general) to reduce the number of legitimate secondary-copies—and thus to minimise the number of exposed **attack-surfaces** (or eliminate the same).

Attaining adequate protection for any illegitimate secondary-copies and/or tertiary-copies; requires specialist data-encryption, plus identity and access management techniques.

And that's about it for now.

We have identified key principles of safe network design. Remaining is to 'explode' said factors; and to bring *visibility, clarity, understanding* and *predictability* to all of the relevant *actors, entities* and *processes*, plus *attack* and *defensive methods*, that may be present/possible.

* * * * *

Access Protection = Provision of:

A. Defence-mechanism(s) to prevent unauthorised access; and
B. Entry method(s) to facilitate valid entry.

Figures 4 & 5: Secure Point-To-Point Communication System

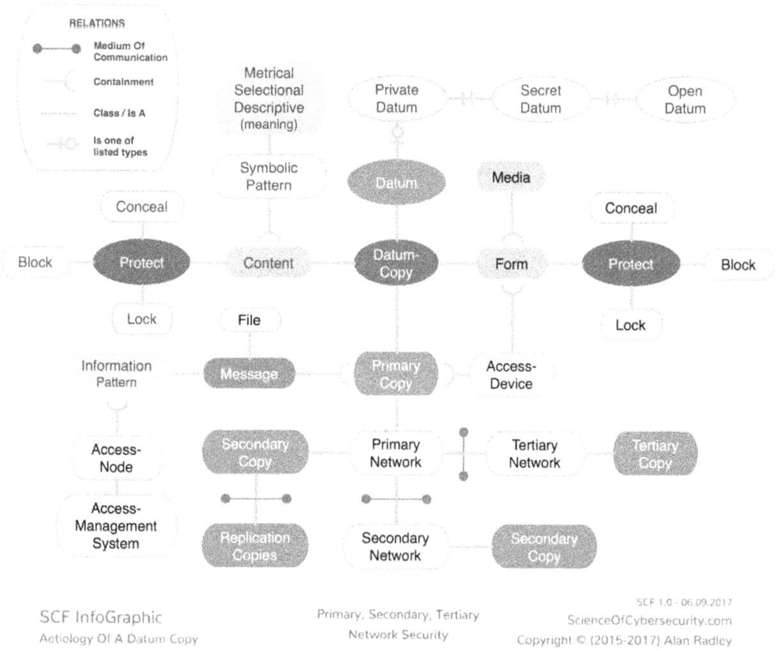

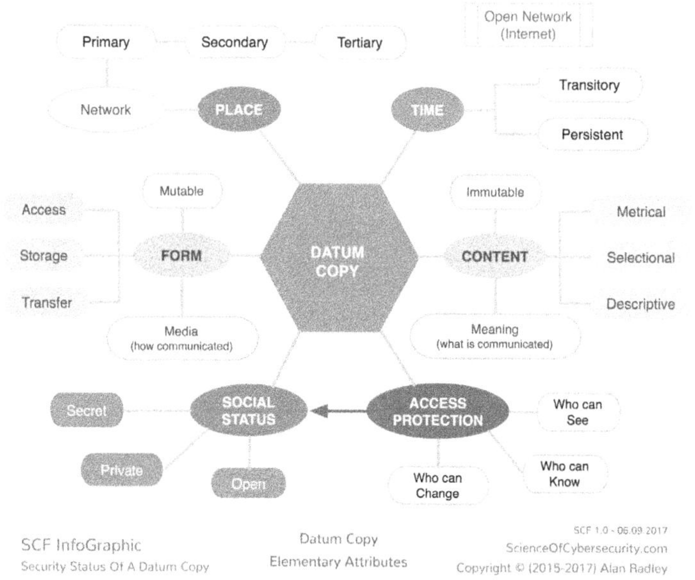

RELATIONS

Medium Of Communication

Containment

Class / Is A

Is one of listed types

The whole notion of passwords is based on an oxymoron. The idea is to have a random string that is easy to remember. Unfortunately, if it's easy to remember, it's something nonrandom like 'Susan.' And if it's random, like 'r7U2*Qnp,' then it's not easy to remember.

— Bruce Schneier

Companies spend millions of dollars on firewalls, encryption and secure access devices, and it's money wasted, because none of these measures address the weakest link in the security chain.

— Kevin Mitnick

Phishing is an example of a particularly interesting hacking technique; whereby when the user clicks on a file thinking it will perform one specific action (e.g. opening a file)—it secretly or overtly does something entirely different! — Radley

A secure system is one that
does what it is supposed to.

— Eugene Spafford

CHAPTER 5

Building Actor Coherent Defences

THE SUBJECT AT hand is the building of *actor-coherent defences*—with respect to the safe transfer of meaning between individual human beings.[12]

Accordingly, we specify a nominal primary-network's data-processing stack; and with a view to obtaining Absolute Security for communicated datum(s).

Security is *protection of privacy (of meaning) for a communicated datum.* Ergo, a second goal of this chapter is to identify—attack-surface/window type(s)—for said private-datum; and by means of logically consistent definitions, analysis and exposition.

---

[12] The OED (2nd Edition) lists the following for the entry 'meaning':

1) That which is intended to be—or actually is—expressed or indicated. Alternatively: 2) Of language, a sentence, word, etc.: The signification, sense, import; a sense, interpretation. Also, 3) the intent, spirit as apart from the 'letter' (of a statement, law, etc.). 4) †(that) is to meaning: (that) means.

The term **data-processing stack** refers to the sum total of all the actors, entities and processes etc; existing on—and/or potentially influencing—a primary-network's communication 'pipeline'. As previously indicated, this stack may involve *hybrid-actors* emanating from outside the primary-network—on secondary/tertiary/open-network(s)—including known and unknown, and desirable and undesirable, ones etc.

How can we get a grip on something so ephemeral?

We begin by identifying (potential) vulnerabilities on a supposedly secure communication 'pipeline'.

Attack-surfaces come in six basic kinds [Axiom 26].

Firstly we have three related to the datum-copy's **form**; or its encapsulating *media of storage, transfer and access.*[13]

Secondly we have three attack-surface types related to the datum-copy's **content;** and these are the *metrical, descriptive* and *selectional* ones.[14]

Locking / Blocking / Concealment

Patently, the generalised locking, blocking and concealment tools/strategies apply not only to items—but also to processes and methods. But remember that these ideas are analysis tools—which may be mixed, interlaced, overlaid etc and so are not sharply defined physical laws!

----

[13] The author has compartmentalised media into three kinds; but as explained later—often real-world media are a combination of two or more types—for example central-server networks—which combine access, transfer and storage functions.

[14] See: **Information, Mechanism and Meaning** (MIT Press—1969) by Donald M. MacKay. Whereby attack-surface types (our concepts) have been equated to Donald's: three kinds of information layer(s) present in any representation.

Unsafe-Actor

An actor (i.e. a program/human/process) existing on and/or influencing the data-processing stack that may be structurally—visible/invisible and/or known/unknown in terms of existence—but remain questionable/harmful in terms of purpose, value, action and/or integrity—and hence may (potentially) cause undetermined/detrimental/harmful effects and/or progress unknown or undesirable programming path(s); or else provide unauthorised access to private-datum(s) etc [Axiom 27].

Whereby the term unsafe-actor encapsulates the meaning(s) of the term **threat-actor/attacker** and similar terminology.

Defensive Mechanism(s)

A datum-copy—encapsulated on a media device—has three components: two related to form: the **physical representation**, and the **virtual representation,** and one related to content: which is the **meaning representation** (with the aforementioned *metrical, descriptive* and *selectional* aspects) [Axiom 28].

Ergo, there are 5 possible attack-surface types for each of three possible media of **storage, transfer** and **access**—leading to a grand total of 15 attack-surface types. However each surface may be protected by 6 kinds of protection (entry-method(s) + defence-method(s)): or **locking, blocking** and **concealment** mechanism(s); hence we can have up to 90 fundamental kinds/types of protection for a single copy (or a private datum existing on a communication(s) security system) [Axiom 29].

Local Actor

A **local-actor** is a data processing unit—existing on a local access-device—comprised of either hardware and/or software/human elements—which (potentially) acts on a datum-copy's form and/or content within the primary-network's data-processing stack [Axiom 30].

Network Actor

A **network-actor** is a data processing unit—existing on a remote networked-device—comprised of either hardware and/or software/human elements—which (potentially) acts on a datum-copy's form and/or content within the primary-network's data-processing stack [Axiom 31].

Actor Coherence

An **actor-coherent defence** is when all of the actors, entities and processes—present in a primary-network's data-processing stack—are *impelled* to act together in order to protect the private datum-copy's form and/or content from unwarranted social access (hopefully for all places/ times) [Axiom 32]. N.B. An actor may originate—from either automated processes and/or human ones.

Access-Node / Access-Device

An **access-node** is a virtual access gateway (i.e. legitimate login-node/point-of-entry) for a primary/secondary/tertiary network; and is normally used (only) by an authorised party to gain entry to said network. An **access-device** is a physical access device that enables a human to gain entry to the same network (i.e. a personal computer) [Axiom 33].

Primary Network

The **primary-network** is a provided point-to-point communication system; whereby a private **access-node** (the source-point) exists on a networked **access-device**; which stores a primary-copy of a private-datum; prior to the single-copy-send of the same to a socially restricted access-node (the destination-point) [Axiom 34]. A primary-network may create legitimate secondary-copies of the primary-copy.

Secondary Network

A **secondary-network** is a privileged-access network intimately connected to the primary-network's communication pipeline; whereby copies of communicated private-datum(s) may exist on an nth-party organisational network and/or various local and/or central replication (backup) network(s) [Axiom 35]. A secondary-network may contain legitimate replicated secondary-copies of primary-copies and/or other secondary-copies.

Tertiary Network

A **tertiary-network** is not directly connected to the primary-network—but nevertheless may still (belatedly) access data traffic flowing across primary and/or secondary-networks—resulting in illegitimate **tertiary-copies** of primary/secondary-copies [Axiom 36].

An *actor-coherent* defence guarantees that all actors present on a primary-network's data-processing stack work-together to protect the privacy of a datum's content.

Two kinds of operational strategies exist for achieving an actor-coherent defence. Firstly, we can attempt to identify **unsafe-actors** and limit their harmful activities—but this may be extremely difficult to do—since actor types are numerous and many are unknown/remote/hidden.

Secondly, we can move all **copies** (or attack-surfaces) beyond the reach of any harmful actors—still a difficult process—but at least the copy types are known—and hence (potentially) defendable. Normally we employ both techniques (to the same effect); but in our thesis we shall emphasise the latter approach—protecting copies from attack.

Illustrated below is a generalised hacking procedure— but bear-in-mind that all defensive strategies relate to protection of either **form** or **content** (for a datum-copy).

Any attack begins with <u>form</u>. Logically, an intruder must possess a means of engaging with (one or more) of the encapsulating: *media of storage, transfer* and/or *access*—for a primary, secondary or tertiary copy. Accordingly, the attacker (and his 'helper' actors) must first connect with the private copy's **physical-representation**—and by opening-up an electronic/magnetic/optical 'container'—in order to obtain a **virtual-representation** of the copy.

––––––

Polymorphic Code / Attack(s)

A polymorphic code is code that uses a polymorphic engine to mutate while keeping the original algorithm intact. That is, the code changes itself each time it runs, but the function of the code (its semantics) will not change at all. For example, 1+3 and 6-2 both achieve the same result while using different code. This technique is sometimes used by computer viruses, shell-codes and computer worms to hide their presence.

Figure 6: Attack-Surface Types (Datum-Copy)

Next because the copy has been transposed into a storage/ transmission/presentation format; the virtual representation must be processed to extract the inner datum(s)—or **meaning-representation** (normally).

Ergo protection of a form based attack-surface—implies preventing/blocking any unsafe-actor(s) from gaining unwarranted access to (opening-up) the physical and/or virtual representation(s) of the copy (see later chapters).

The next task is to extract **meaning** from datum content. Remember that a representation has metrical, descriptive and selectional aspects. Notably, the metrical aspect—or pattern of atomic facts/symbols—is always present—and works together with a descriptive aspect—to convey meaning.

The so-called **metrical attack-surface** may be protected (for example) by means of encryption *(entry locks + content concealment)*—or obfuscation of symbolic structure—and so that only an actor with the correct unlocking algorithm(s)/key(s) can decode the underlying symbolic pattern [Axiom 37].

Once the metrical layer is decoded, we must match each symbol to its specific meaning—and according to the common descriptive language employed—named the **descriptive attack-surface** [Axiom 38]. Notably the sender and receiver may be using an obscure coding language whereby the symbol-to-meaning relationship is protected (i.e. **RED** means **BIG** etc). Finally, modal context(s)—named **selectional attack-surface(s)**—may protect constructive aspect(s) of the representation [Axiom 39].

Do not worry if this chapter seems overly theoretical—all will become clear soon enough—because we are now in possession of all the principles needed to specify Absolute Security [ref. Absolute Security: TARGET and METHOD(S)]. [15]

* * * * *

Confusion/Obfuscation: Multiple Layers of Meaning (Metrical, Descriptive, Selectional)—Within a representation, multiple layers of meaning may be present, and/or be overlaid in confusing packetized space/time formats, and/or be ordered seemingly out-of-sequence, and/or be applied as in a 'Russian-Doll' fashion.

---

[15] In this book, we focus on identification of first-principles for privacy/security—as opposed to mathematical explanations and/or low-level system design constructs. See Chapter 1: Definition of Absolute Security.

Concealment

We have the **target** (item to be concealed); and the concealment **method**. Whereby there are two basic kinds of concealment structural targets: **existence** of the item, and **content** (or inner meaning) [Axiom 40].

Structure can be—CONCEALED—in 3 ways [Axiom 41]:

A. Conceal **form** itself; or

B. Conceal **location (where)**; or

C. Conceal **location (when)**: item time-span, duration or persistence.

Whereby there are 3 basic processes [Axiom 42]:
(for each method/way)

A. Conceal by *transformation* of form/location; or

B. Conceal by *similarity (equivalency)*—that is by hiding an item alongside a large number (of ostensibly identical) items; and

C. Conceal by *difference (complexity)*—or hiding an item amongst a large number of greatly/potentially varying forms/structures.

N.B. Concealment/camouflaging of a system access gateway—is a one-time technique (for an individual gateway), hence you cannot reanimate it after the first failure—as opposed to key expiration whereby you simply throw it away and get a new one.

———

Code-words and Code-groups

In communication, a code-word/code-group is an element of a standardised code or protocol. Each code-word/group is assembled in accordance with the specific rules of the code and assigned a unique meaning. Code-words are typically used for reasons of *reliability, clarity, brevity, and/or secrecy.*

Attack Surface / Window

An **attack-surface/attack-window** is an exposed facet/ system entry-point for a datum-copy, existing on a primary-network's data-processing stack, and which (potentially) facilitates unwarranted social access to a private datum-copy's content and/or form [Axiom 43].

Attack Vector

An **attack-vector** is a specific data-processing path, existing on a primary-network's data-processing stack—which (potentially) provides unwarranted social access to a private datum-copy's content and/or form [Axiom 44].

Security System Exploit

An **exploit** is a piece of software, a chunk of data, or a sequence of commands that takes advantage of a bug or vulnerability (via a poorly-protected Access Gateway) in order to cause unintended or unanticipated behavior to occur on a computer system's software, hardware, or something electronic.

Access Gateway

An **access-gateway** consists of one or more access-nodes and/or exposed attack-surface(s)/window(s)—for a primary, secondary or tertiary copy [Axiom 45]. The gateway is comprised of a group of hardware/software elements that together form an 'entrance aperture' for actor pathway(s).

The gateway may be—open or shut—visible or invisible— protected or unprotected—at any particular place/time— and for specific actor(s)/attack-vector(s)—and by means of **access/locking mechanism(s)**.

Representation Aspects

We have characterised a datum-copy—as a representation consisting of three aspects: firstly the **physical-representation** (or encapsulating media of storage, transfer and access for the datum-copy); and secondly the **virtual-representation** (datum-copy in a storage, transfer, and/or access format); and finally the **meaning-representation** (a datum with metrical, descriptive and selectional layers).

All three representation layers/aspects are not-necessarily present/protected for a particular copy. For example, you can have a physical-representation—but no format (meaningless data). Or else a copy with encrypted metrical structure (i.e. locked + concealed); but no unusual descriptive structure(s), that also uses standard modeless structure(s)—hence no descriptive/selective protection.

———

Security by Obscurity: 'Incidentally, it did occur to me that the whole CVE disclosure process shows how reliant we currently are on security by obscurity (that is so frowned on by experts). Our unintentional and unavoidable reliance on it will continue to be our main and implicit defence until we find a way to write software that is inherently automatically secure.'

— Personal communication from Nigel Pugh (February 17th 2016) [see CVE]

How long before we see all kinds of underground and illicit new Internet communication systems—like TOR—which use their own packet routing protocols and unbreakable defense systems—and to escape oversight? — Radley

Data exfiltration is the unauthorised transfer of sensitive information from a target's network to a location which a threat actor controls. Because data routinely moves in and out of networked enterprises, data exfiltration can closely resemble normal network traffic, making detection of exfiltration attempts challenging for IT security groups. — Radley

Malicious Code: Software (e.g., Trojan horse) that appears to perform a useful or desirable function, but actually gains unauthorised access to system resources or tricks a user into executing other malicious logic.

Masquerade Attack: A type of attack in which one system entity illegitimately poses as (assumes the identity of) another entity.

Nothing stops you placing lots of chains around your safe.
— Radley

CHAPTER 6

Primary Network Design

THE SUBJECT AT hand is the design of a *primary-network*—with respect to the safe transfer of meaning between individual human beings.

Accordingly, we specify the component(s) of a nominal primary network's data-processing stack; and with a view to obtaining Absolute Security for communicated datum(s) [ref. Absolute Security:TARGET].

A second goal of this chapter is to identify safe principles of design/operation—for a primary—network—and by means of logically consistent definitions, analysis and exposition.[16]

---

[16] A quick reminder of purpose is useful; because in this book, we are simply attempting to define: **Absolute Security (see Chapter 1).**

A quick glance at the word '**define**'; in the OED (2nd Edition); provides the following listings: 1) To bring to an end. To bring to an end (a controversy, etc.); 2) to determine, decide, settle. 3) To determine the boundary or spatial extent of; to settle the limits of. Also 4) To determine, lay down definitely; to fix, decide; to decide upon, fix upon; and 5) To state precisely or determinately; to specify.

Media Types

A **storage-media** is a bundle of hardware/software technologies that work together to form a memory system—and in order to persist a datum-copy's form and content [Axiom 46]. Example types include: hard disc drives, solid state drives, optical drives, magnetic drives, and cloud storage systems like Dropbox, iCloud, and Google-Drive etc.

A **transfer-media** is a bundle of hardware/software technologies that work together to form a delivery system—and in order to send a datum-copy from a source-point to a destination-point [Axiom 47]. Example types include any data transfer system consisting of telecommunication components such as wired and/or wireless links, data channels etc; including low level protocols such as LAN, WAN, FTP, HTTP and high level protocols like email etc. The definition would include networked applications like DropBox, Google-Drive etc.

An **access-media** is a hardware/software system that enables an actor to *see, know* and/or *change* a copy's form and/or content (e.g. a data-access terminal) [Axiom 48].

N.B. Real-world media are normally an amalgamation of all three media types—**storage, transfer** and **access**. However blending media types/functions unnecessarily can be a source of security problems. For example, any superfluous mixing of the transfer and storage functions—may lead to exposed datum-copies at undesirable place(s)/time(s). In our terms, it is a question of how best to preserve socially secure communication.

In previous chapters we emphasised the need to bring *actor-coherence* to a primary-network's defences; and in terms of protecting the **data-processing stack** from the unwarranted activities of any unsafe-actors (i.e. automated and/or human ones).

Accordingly, it is useful to identify the specific features of a nominal attack-surface, which (in any way) relate to exposure of a private-datum's form and/or content.

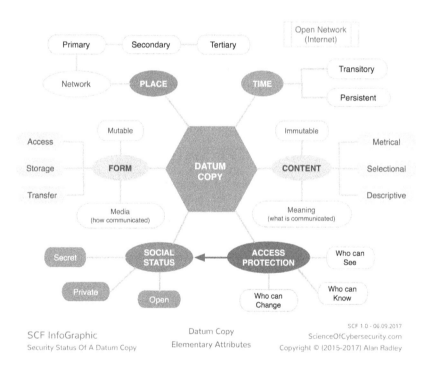

Figure 7: Attack Surface as Datum-Copy

THE SCIENCE OF CYBERSECURITY

Concealment Target

There are basically two kinds of concealment targets; you can either focus on concealing structure—or else encourage the observer to look elsewhere (still a form of concealment) [Axiom 49].

Whereby either the onlooker:

A. Does not know **where** or **when** to look for an item (target location obfuscation); or secondly:

B. Finds that looking does not reveal **how** to find the item (target form confusion); or finally:

C. Is encouraged to look **elsewhere** than an item's true location (observer misdirection—i.e. concentrate on directing the attention of the observer—using decoys and/or false targets—or hide messages in innocuous content etc).

CVE System

CVE Identifiers: The Common Vulnerabilities and Exposures (CVE) system provides a reference-method for publicly known information-security vulnerabilities and exposures. The MITRE Corporation's documentation defines CVE Identifiers as unique, common identifiers for publicly known information-security vulnerabilities in publicly released software packages. The National Cybersecurity FFRDC, owned by The MITRE Corporation, maintains the system, with funding from the National Cyber Security Division of the United States Department of Homeland Security. CVE is used by the Security Content Automation Protocol, and CVE IDs are listed on MITRE's system as well as the US National Vulnerability Database.

Masquerade Attack

A type of attack in which one system entity illegitimately poses as (assumes the identity of) another entity.

Copies and Attack-Surfaces

In this book, we have characterised all attack-surfaces as being (in one way or another) equivalent to an exposed datum-copy. In one respect—this is correct—and because any (successfully exploited) attack-surface must provide a pathway to a copy—and thus can be equated to an exposed facet of the copy—as it comes to exist on the communication system.

However in another sense—it is obvious that not all attack-surfaces are copies—for example system-logins (access-nodes), access-devices, plus exposed communication data and encryption keys etc—are all (potentially) illicit windows into the system that may allow an unsafe-actor to access a *primary*, *secondary* or *tertiary* copy.

Copy at-Rest / in-Transit

A datum-copy which is **at-rest** has a physical form that (normally) exists as an integrated unit of static information —because it has been memory 'saved' on an electronic storage media. Conversely, a datum-copy that is **in-transit** is moving (and possibly segmented) across a telecommunications line etc.

A physical-gateway defines a set of possible entry-method(s) for 'grasping' a digital-copy; and examples include valid and invalid access-nodes (logins), illicit software CVE break-ins, (successful entry-method(s): viruses, trojans, hacking etc), plus stolen CDs, hard-drives, and computers etc; including any and all ways of obtaining access to the container—or outer form—of the copy.

We can begin by characterising an attack-surface as equivalent to an exposed datum-copy (see Figure-7).

For Absolute Security, we must protect:

A. **Physical-Gateway(s)**—who can obtain a physical copy.

B. **Virtual-Gateway(s)**—who can open a virtual copy.

C. **Meaning-Gateway(s)**—who can decode datum(s).

To be successful, an intruder must first pass through the physical and virtual gateway(s); prior to deciphering the meaning of the inner datum(s)—or passing through any meaning-gateway(s) that happen to be present [Axiom 50].

Obviously a variety of different kinds of primary-network designs are possible—each with a specific feature set; but which one is safest? In order to find out—we can take a step-by-step approach to protecting access-gateway(s) for a nominal network.

In terms of securing **physical-gateway(s)**—or *locking/ blocking/concealing*—all access-gateways/pathways related to the copy's physical representation—we can (perhaps) begin by eliminating all legitimate secondary-copies. This can be done by moving to a **Peer-to-Peer (P2P)** network (no central copies)—assuming that no other organisational/transfer/replicated copies exist on any secondary-network(s) (see later chapters).

Next we can focus on removing any possibility of an unwarranted nth-party producing illegitimate secondary/tertiary-copies. Here we rely on securing the datum's content during live transport.

Special line-encryption/packet-scrambling methods can be used *(transport locks)*, in addition to moving the communication channel out-of-reach of an attacker—by means of closed physical and/or concealed **virtual-gateway(s)** *(blocking/existence concealment)*.

For example, we can use invisible/transitory access-node(s); **secret** protocol(s), **private** servers/ packet-routing mechanism(s); and/or employ **covert** access-device(s) with hidden/spoofed **IP/MAC** data.

Remaining is a single class of attack-surface—primary-copies. In some ways this type of attack-surface is the most difficult to protect; because an access-device/node is analogous to an armour reinforced bank vault.

Whereby once an attacker is inside the vault—he/she (normally) has free access to all of the valuable items. Unfortunately there are many ways for an attacker to break into this type of 'vault'—or access-node/device.

Normally we must rely on a mishmash collection of (protected) physical/virtual gateways provided by network administrators, system manufactures etc.

However due to the evolving nature of the risk; including newly discovered exploit(s), uncertain attack-vector(s) and countless hostile actor(s) etc; it is difficult to secure each access-node with full confidence over an extended period of time. One way to mitigate against such risk(s) is to move the access-node (plus associated private-copies/data-set(s))— beyond the reach of an attacker.

Ergo, we protect all entry-method(s)—with valid access control(s) plus advanced encryption—that is—by locking all **virtual/meaning-gateways**.

Another way is to move the same to a secure portable device—with hidden **IP/MAC** addresses (i.e. closing/blocking/concealing all **physical gateways**).

In summary, **access-gateways** (for datum-copies) can be classified into three kinds: *physical-gateways, virtual-gateways* and *meaning-gateways.*

Ergo gateway defences are predicated upon one—or more—of the following factors:

- Unbreakable (or strong) encryption/coding for copies;
- Secure Entity/Access/ID: Management System(s);
- 'Stealth' network design features.

All three predicates assume a primary-network with unimpeachable operations that provides socially secure communication for shared datum(s).

Ergo, we know *what* is required for Absolute Security—next we must prescribe *how.*

* * * * *

The Hacker's Advantage

Unfortunately, even a single hacked entry-method or exploited attack-surface—can lead to a data-breach that effectively invalidates all the other protective mechanisms. An attacker has to be successful just once (in relation to any number of attacks); whereas a defender must successfully protect datum(s) for each and every attack, or maintain a 100 percent success rate—forever!

Zero Day Vulnerability—A zero day vulnerability refers to a hole in software that is unknown to the vendor. This security hole is then exploited by hackers before the vendor becomes aware and hurries to fix it—this exploit is called a **zero day attack.**

CHAPTER 7

Encryption Theory

THE SUBJECT AT hand is protection of *metrical attack-surface(s)*; with respect to the safe transfer of meaning between individual human beings.

Accordingly, we specify how to protect symbolic structure (for datum(s)); and with a view to obtaining unbreakable encryption for datum-copies.

A second goal of this chapter is to define and classify encryption mechanism(s) for primary-network defence (i.e. locking datum-copies)—by means of logically consistent definitions, analysis and exposition.[17]

---

[17] N.B. Whilst in this book we have apparently overlooked **Identity and Access Management Systems**—plus **Secret-Key Management/Identity Authentication/Validation Techniques**—this is not so—and because most of the security and privacy techniques listed here which relate to the safe: transfer/storage/access of datum(s)—apply also to User-IDs, passwords, entity-identification, logins and Keys etc. Additionally, the problem of identity/key assurance is cyclic/nested in nature—whereby one has to either trust the (nth-party) party supplying/approving the item—or else defer to yet another (trusted) authority. Ultimately, it is the user himself who approves a party—or source/destination point—and/or a copy/key/certificate—by implicitly/explicitly trusting a particular validation method.

Semiotic Theory

In semiotics a **sign** is something that can be interpreted as having a meaning, which is something other than itself, and which is therefore able to communicate information to the one interpreting or decoding the sign.

Charles Peirce (1839-1914) developed a triadic theory of semiotics in which a sign is—a relation between the **sign-vehicle** (the physical form of the sign), a **sign-object** (the aspect of the world that the sign carries meaning about), and an **interpretant** (the meaning of the sign as understood by the interpreter).

Icons, Indices, Symbols

Signs are either icons, indices or symbols. **Icons** signify by means of similarity between sign vehicle and sign object (e.g. a map), **indices** signify by means of a direct relation of contiguity or causality between sign vehicle and sign object (e.g. a symptom), and **symbols** signify through a law or social convention (i.e letters/words present in a language).

———

End-to-End Encryption (ETEE) is a system of communication where only the people communicating can read the messages. No eavesdropper can access the cryptographic keys needed to decrypt the conversation, including telecom providers, Internet providers and the company that runs the messaging service (theoretically).

ETEE example = Encrypt data at source with personal/user-owned key.

Hybrid Encryption—An application of cryptography that combines two or more encryption algorithms, particularly a combination of symmetric and asymmetric encryption.

Lock / Block / Conceal

[Access Protection Mechanism(s)]

It is possible that you may experience confusion—in relation to the application of the three protective methods—*lock*, *block* and *conceal*—to the safeguarding of a datum-copy. Just for clarification—herein whenever we speak of a <u>locking</u> mechanism for a datum-copy (existing on a specific media of storage, transfer and access)—what we are saying is that the **lock** prevents the **knowing/opening action** (i.e for datum access)—by some protected entry-method plus defence-method(s) (i.e. password entry-system (lock) plus content concealment of symbolic structure) [Axiom 51.1].

Alternatively, **existence <u>concealment</u>** prevents an unsafe-actor from **seeing/finding a copy** by means of an entry-method that is itself secret/hidden (i.e. unusual descriptive coding) and/or secret/hidden defence-method(s) (e.g. possibly identical to entry-method) [Axiom 51.2].

Likewise for <u>blocking</u> **actions** (ref. reaching) [Axiom 51.2].

Obviously there is overlap (and nesting) between the concepts of lock, block and conceal—but it is often useful to open-up protection—as a concept—into such facets.

———

CODE (French, Latin: 'tree-trunk', 'writing tablet')—A method of concealment that may use words, numbers or syllables to replace original words/phrases of a message. Codes substitute whole words whereas ciphers transpose or substitute letters or digi-graphs. Also a disguised way of evoking meaning (non-symbolic obfuscation).

The topic at hand is creation of an impenetrable **meaning-gateway**—or protecting a datum-copy's metrical attack-surface (or symbolic structure)—whereby the same copy is either—A) *at-rest*; or B) *in-transit.*

Wherein we assume that any physical and/or virtual getaways (or protective measures for the copy's form) may be ineffective and/or could fail.

Right away—for a point-to-point communication system connected to an open-network—we acknowledge that a problem exists in terms of message/identity/key: authentication and signification; or making certain that the *Identity and Access Management System* assigns the same to the correct party.

Placing these matters aside, we find that there are two basic kinds of symbolic encryption:

- *Symmetric-Key-Encryption:* the encryption and decryption keys are the same. Communicating parties must have the same key before they can achieve secure communication.

- *Public-Key-Encryption:* the (public) encryption key is published for anyone to use and encrypt messages. However, only the receiving party has access to the (private) decryption key that allows messages to be read.

———

Cypher-Alphabet

An alphabet composed of substitutes for the normal alphabet or the particular alphabet in which the cipher is written.

Entry-Method / Defence-Method (ref. Datum-Copy)

An entry-method is a system access pathway—or series of actions that must be performed by a human, running program and/or helper actor(s)—to access a datum-copy (i.e. a primary, secondary, tertiary-copy). Whereby an **entry-method** (may) involve traversing several system gateway(s)—before opening up the datum's inner meaning.

A defence-method is a system access pathway that is inaccessible to unsafe-actor(s). Wherein both the **entry-method** and **defence-method(s)** may be protected by *locking*, *blocking* and/or *concealment techniques*.

Note that an entry-method plus defence-method— may sometimes be the exact same sub-subsystem (i.e fulfil a dual purpose for any particular access pathway or system entrance method).

Either symmetric/non-symmetric encryption may be used to develop effective cryptographic software—and standards are widely available for employing such techniques (see end notes and bibliography).

However successfully using encryption to ensure security may be a challenging problem—and because even a single error in system design or execution can allow successful attacks. Sometimes an adversary can obtain unencrypted information without directly undoing the encryption (see the **Trojan Horse/Traffic Analysis** hacking method(s) as explained elsewhere).

Overall, we advise caution in terms of reliance on cryptography alone for protecting a datum's privacy.

In this chapter we are concerned with protection of *symbolic structure*—or meaning—for communicated datum(s); whereby the message is comprised of a specific pattern of symbols. Wherein we ignore the possibility of using *icons* and *indices* as signifiers—and because these topics are unusual and/or lie outside of our analysis (e.g. steganography).

Obviously the remaining topic of *symbolic cryptography* is complex; and any adequate treatment would run to a book-length treatise. How then, you may ask, is it possible in only a few pages to say anything consequential on such a highly technical subject matter? [See page 86 for the answer(s)]

———

Confidentiality

The OED (2nd Edition)—lists for **Confidential:**

1) Of the nature of confidence; spoken or written in confidence; characterised by the communication of secrets or private matters.

2) **Confidential communication:** a communication made between parties who stand in a confidential relation to each other, and therefore privileged in law. Confidential relation: the relation existing between a lawyer and his client, between guardian and ward.

———

Securing a computer system has traditionally been a battle of wits: the penetrator tries to find the holes, and the designer tries to close them.

— Gosser

Cryptography

Cryptography is defined as a secret manner of writing, either by arbitrary characters in other than the ordinary sense, or by methods intelligible only to those possessing a (private) key.

Symbolic Encryption is the process of encrypting symbolic messages—or obfuscating datums consisting of patterns of symbols.[18] Whereby information is encoded in such a way that only authorised parties can read it—typically by replacing/jumbling symbols according to a mathematical procedure which obscures the original symbolic pattern. In an encryption scheme, the intended communication of information, referred to as plaintext (i.e "Alan is tall"), is encrypted using a special algorithm, generating cipher-text that can only be read if decrypted (i.e. "Bmbo jl umm"). For technical reasons, an encryption scheme (for a metrical attack-surface) normally uses a pseudo-random encryption key generated by an algorithm. It is in principle possible to decrypt the message without possessing the key, but, for a well-designed encryption scheme, large computational resources and skill are required. An authorised party can easily decrypt the symbolic message with the key provided by the originator to recipients, but not to unauthorised parties.

---

[18] Wherein we use the term **'symbolic encryption'** in a subtly different manner than in the normal sense; whereby we make a distinction between **cryptography** and **coding**. Ergo, we define a **cypher** as a—secret way of writing by means of unusual structures-of-symbols (symbolic obfuscation)—or the straightforward 'jumbling/transposition' and/or 'replacement/substitution' of letters and words in (for example)—a text message—and according to an 'encryption' algorithm. Whereas we define **coding**—as a disguised way of writing—by means of the assignment of unusual coded meanings for words/concepts/sentences—or employing standard/unusual symbols which map to non-standard ideas structures/datum-meaning(s) (i.e non-symbolic obfuscation).

N.B. Any communication instance has twin aspects: 1) Message conveyance (transfer of symbolic structure or metrical content); and 2) Mapping to underlying facts/datum-meaning(s)—or descriptive content. Of-course the two aspects can overlap and inter-penetrate—but it is often useful to separate the two.

Quite simply, we can identify best practice in terms of logical premises/reasoning/appropriate-conclusions for achieving Absolute Security; and hence outline effective methods to protect the metrical structure of communicated datum(s).

Ergo, we abide by one (or more) of the following— CRYPTOGRAPHIC PRINCIPLES [Axiom 52]:

Principle A

Virtual Message Tamper-proofing: The digital signature verification and *encryption* must be applied to the cipher-text— *when it is created*—typically on the same primary-network used to compose the message—to avoid tampering (adequate locking—guarantees message integrity).

Principle B

Physical Message Tamper-proofing: Encrypting at the time of creation is only secure if the encryption device itself has not been tampered with (i.e. closed/blocked physical gateway(s) or device-integrity).

Principle C

Employ Secret Keys: Obey Dr Claude Shannon's maxim (i.e. Kerckhoff's principle); and assume that: '*the enemy knows the system*'. Avoid relying on *security through obscurity* and/or *security through minority*—in terms of **not** assuming that the secrecy/uncommonness of system design provides unimpeachable protection (adequate concealment + locking).

Principle D

Pattern Obfuscation: Special encryption/coding/scrambling methods must be employed to prevent spies from deducing information from patterns present in the copy.

Principle E

Access-node/Key/ID Security: Adequate access control methods must be employed to protect unwarranted access to any and all access-nodes, access-devices, keys, user IDs etc (adequate blocking + key concealment).

Principle F

Viruses, Trojan-Horses: Methods to eradicate Viruses and to prohibit Trojans misrepresenting as safe-actors—hence preventing unsafe-actors from gaining unwarranted access to copies/actors on the data-processing stack (adequate blocking).

Principle G

Environmental Spying: Methods to prevent spying on the primary-network through leaking emanations, including radio or electrical signals and vibration(s) etc.

*****

The history of cryptography provides evidence that it is difficult to keep details of a widely used algorithm secret.

Accordingly, only secrecy of the key provides sufficient security—and because a key is often easier to protect (it's typically a small piece of information) than an encryption algorithm, and easier to change if compromised.

(N.B. See later chapters for the *defence-in-depth*—or CASTLE—approach to comprehensive information security.)

And that's about it for now; in later chapters we go on to explore all of the issues raised here; and in terms of attaining *logical, holistic, effective* and *broadly considered* (*plus scientific*) Cybersecurity policies.

* * * * *

Comprehensive Information Security

—or Complete Information Security—is an approach to information security that takes a broad-ranging view of, and rigorous approach to, the subject; and places the CIA triad of **confidentiality**, **integrity** and **availability** at the heart of information security policy. These three factors are referred to interchangeably in the literature as security attributes, properties, security goals, fundamental aspects, information criteria, critical information characteristics and basic building blocks etc.

Confidential Information Security

—or Transmissions Security—is an approach to information security that attempts to avoid detection—in terms of usage/application— and by means of special stealth and/or primary-network design features that camouflage any and all communications data from any unauthorised observers. An electronic form of communication security similar to steganography. Transmission security tries to hide the existence of secret messages in electrical exchanges, whether or not they are encrypted. Towards this end—the communication system and related method(s), plus primary-network, communication(s) data, and meta-data etc; are all rendered invisible/undetectable.

––––––––

Jargon-Codes—Open methods of linguistic concealment. A type of open code, the jargon code is not hidden by symbols or transposed letters. Rather, an innocent word or words replaces another term in a sentence constructed in an innocuous fashion.

Beholder's Share

Art historian Sir Earnest Gombrich (1909-2001) first defined the *'beholder's share'*—which states that our perceptual experience—depends on the active interpretation of sensory input. Perception becomes a generative act, one in which biological and sociocultural influences conspire to shape the brain's 'best guess' of the causes (and meaning) of its sensory signals—or in our terms the meaning of the symbolic message being communicated.

Language

A **language** is a systematic way to express thoughts, feelings and ideas; often defined as the whole body of words and methods of words used by a nation, people, race or 'tongue'.

Codes

In our lives we constantly send messages that consist of different signs. These messages are based on **codes**—culturally defined systems of relationships/rules that connect ideas together in pre-defined/socially-agreed ways. Barthes claimed that there is "*no message without a code*".

Safe Metaphor

A **Safe** is a receptacle for the secure storage of items; and any safe has twin aspects; firstly an enclosed space completely covered by an enveloping barrier or unbroken set of armour-reinforced walls—and thus protecting any contained item(s); and secondly a **Lock** and **Key**—which is a method for fastening an entrance aperture into the enclosed space—whereby the lock is a sealed entrance aperture—or a mechanism for restricting access to only those persons who actually possess and may use the key to unlock the same aperture. In our terms—the (lock + key) represents a valid entry-method enabling an actor to traverse a system access gateway; and the (safe + lock) is part of the defence mechanism(s) employed by the communication system to prevent access to the same gateway by any unsafe-actors.

Forward-Secrecy / Perfect-Secrecy

In cryptography, **forward secrecy** is a property of secure communication protocols; a secure communication protocol is said to have **forward secrecy** if compromise of long-term keys does not compromise past session keys. This means that the compromise of one message cannot compromise others as well, and there is no one secret value whose acquisition would compromise multiple messages.

Forward secrecy can be achieved by A) using new keys for each communication instance; or B) using multi-layered encryption—and hiding long-term keys inside a layer protected by short-terms keys (other methods are possible).

Perfect secrecy is when an encrypted message (or cypher-text) reveals absolutely nothing about the unencrypted message (or plaintext). Perfect secrecy is obviously a very difficult (if not impossible) feature to achieve in a practical system (see one-time-pads).

Protection by Diversity is a fundamental principle for attaining secrecy/privacy; whereby we first block/bar entry to a private item by some defensive means or protective barrier. Next we build a window/door into the barrier that may be opened (i.e. know/open action)—but only by means of a fully/partially secret entry-method. The entry-method typically includes a mathematical/text value and/or locking key (i.e. a secret password) with a specific form known/available only to authorised parties—and that is difficult to attain/guess; whereby it is diversity (potential to have many different values) that protects the key from discovery/use by an attacker [Axiom 53].

Open-Codes—A code concealed in an apparently innocent message. Open codes are a branch of linguistically masked communications which includes null cyphers, geometric methods and jargon codes.

CHAPTER 8

The Beholder's Share

(Unbreakable Codes)

THE SUBJECT AT hand is protection of *descriptive* and *selectional* attack-surface(s)—with respect to the safe transfer of meaning between individual human beings.

Accordingly, we specify how to protect descriptive structure (for datum(s)); and with a view to obtaining Absolute Security for communicated datum-copy(s).

A second goal of this chapter is to define and classify coding mechanism(s) for primary-network defence—by means of logically consistent definitions, analysis and exposition.[19]

---

[19] Philosophically speaking, when we turn our attention to the **Beholder's Share**—or the interpretive contribution of the observer (aka sender/receiver)—two vital aspects come to mind: 1) firstly, we have to admit that interpretation is always present (to a smaller or greater degree), and because it is the observer herself who determines/assigns meaning (ultimately) to a representation; and also 2): we cannot have protection of privacy without: A) in some way causing (aspects of) the interpretation (ref. encryption/coding) to remain a secret known only to sender/receiver; and also B) we must align the interpretative contribution(s) of both sender/receiver perfectly.

Descriptive / Selective Coding

Descriptive coding refers to the process of assigning a pattern of symbols to the specific meaning of the conveyed message (communicated datum(s)) [Axiom 54.1]. For a message with no descriptive attack-surface; typically a common (or well-known) descriptive language is employed—and in order to achieve effective (open) communication. However when the sender/receiver wish to communicate privately (i.e. using single-copy-send); then unusual symbol-meaning relationships (codes) and/or mappings can be employed. Typically use of a secret look-up-table/coding-method is desirable—for example sending numbers instead of words—whereby the numbers (uniquely) match to a specific page off-set, line-offset, and word-position in (for example) the Bible. Wherein coding numbers begin/continue/end on pre-identified page(s) known only to the sender/receiver.

Selective coding refers to the process of protecting constructive aspects of the symbolic and/or descriptive components of the message by means of private modal context(s) [Axiom 54.2]. There are a near infinite range of coding techniques for so doing; whereby the sender and receiver use an agreed coding mode according to some pre-agreed indices. An example of combined descriptive plus selective coding—is sending the message "Alan is tall": in the form of the number sets: (1, 67, 14, 3); (6, 13, 2,7); (56,3,107,23); wherein each set refers to: secret look-up-table, page, line, and word-number.

Dictionary Attack: An attack that tries all of the phrases or words in a dictionary, trying to crack a password or key. A dictionary attack uses a predefined list of words compared to a brute force attack that tries all possible combinations.

Hybrid Attack: A Hybrid Attack builds on the dictionary attack method by adding numerals and symbols to dictionary words.

The topic at hand is creation of impenetrable **descriptive** and **selectional gateway(s)**—or protecting a datum-copy's descriptive and selectional attack-surface(s) (i.e. defining language(s) used and/or coding structure(s) employed). Whereby the same copy is either—A) *at-rest;* or B) *in-transit.* Wherein we assume that any *physical, virtual,* plus (symbolic) *meaning* gateway(s)—may be ineffective and/or could fail.

Once again we are faced with a host of potentially valid techniques in terms of *descriptive* and *selective* coding. The large number of such combinations makes for a particularly useful set of protective measures—each with a high level of robustness and immunity to attack.

Whereby the *large number and great diversity of potential coding method(s)* helps to effectively cloak/obscure—said attack surface(s); and because an attacker has difficulty guessing which specific protective technique(s) may have been used—leading to significant obstacle(s) for breaking into the coded datum(s).

However there is an important caveat here, in terms of any unbridled optimism with respect to coding methods.

That is the susceptibility of all coding/encryption methods to attacks—whereby a spy attempts to *deduce information* from patterns present in the copy.

We can think of coding as a statistical technique. Ergo for any fairly long message of—for example—english text; if a consistent encryption and/or coding method is employed; then due to the (relatively) small range of letters/words/phrases present in the english language—it may be possible to use numerical/computationally intensive methods to discover, guess and/or decode the original message.

We can conclude that no coding/encryption method is (by itself) absolutely secure against all possible attack-vectors.[20] Ergo, form based protection is desirable. Previously, we had identified core principles of system design for symbolic cryptography. Here in this chapter we wish to do the same for *coding methods*—defined as the generation of descriptive and/or selectional layers for a representation.

Note that we can also use special coding techniques and/or modal methods for protecting symbolic structure—but we normally assign the same to encryption as a topic in-and-of-itself.

Right away we shall state that all of the vulnerabilities and principles for effective cryptography apply also to coding methods. The only difference is that coding methods may be superior for eliminating and/or reducing the possibility of an attacker deducing information from well-known and/or repeated patterns (i.e. phrases) present in the communicated datum.

Pattern obfuscation is a central concern in terms of achieving *socially secure communication*. Basically we are in the domain of statistics—because no matter how clever/intricate and/or obscure the coding or encryption technique—it can often be broken—given sufficient time, effort and resources.

Note however, that to break into a protected datum using statistical methods requires that a sufficiently large— homogenous coded-segment—or section of cypher-text/ coded-text sample is available for analysis.

---

[20] An exception to this rule might be the use of One-Time-Pads.

Ergo we wish to avoid: using identical natural-language constructs too-often in a long message; and/or use of the same coding method(s) continually.

Plus we wish to avoid sending coded messages with common patterns that may be used to reverse-engineer the coded datum(s). In fact, this is how the German **Enigma** code was broken; whereby every message contained known words—'Heil Hitler'—day after day.[21]

How can we mitigate such formidable risks? Quite simply, by using sufficiently obscure and intricate descriptive coding schemes and/or strong encryption methods; plus by using selectional content that varies sufficiently in terms of modal obfuscation.

———

Rights Management

In the digital realm the concept of a copy—unlike a physical copy existing in the real-world—can be a perfect copy of the original (in form/content)—apart from the location at which the copy resides. Contrasted with everyday objects, the question of which copy is the real one arises; in addition to related questions like ownership protection and who has the publication rights etc. Ergo, in the digital world there may (in a sense) no longer be an original or true copy. These issues are often very difficult to resolve/determine—and may involve vast resources and sophisticated technical means, that are (for example) required to protect any private copy which exists in the public arena (ref. movies, music etc).

---

[21] The Enigma machines were a series of electro-mechanical rotor cipher machines developed in the early to mid-twentieth century to protect German commercial, diplomatic and military communications.

Ergo—for socially secure communication—we abide by—as many as possible of—the following message/datum—CODING PRINCIPLES [Axiom 55]:

A. Employ effective *symbolic encryption;* including multi-layer encryption with new keys generated for each communication instance (i.e. use *perfect-forward-secrecy*).

B. Employ obscure *descriptive coding* methods (i.e. one-time-pad(s) or *perfect-secrecy*).

C. Employ variable *selectional coding* methods (i.e. multiple code-books in a single message); with constantly changing constructive pattern(s) for each message. (i.e. one-time-pad(s) or *perfect-secrecy*).

D. Employ *safe pattern constructs.* Avoid sending identical (coded) natural-language constructs repetitively; pad the pattern(s) with NULLS or hide them; use varying constructive code(s).

E. Rely on the *Beholder's Share*—employ covert and obscure methods for interpretation of meaning.

———

And that's about it for now; in the next chapter we explain—form based—defensive gateways.

★ ★ ★ ★ ★

The Cake Is A Lie

YOU CAN BAKE A CAKE WITHOUT SUGAR AND NOBODY WILL NOTICE, UNTIL THEY ACTUALLY TRY IT. BY THEN IT'S TOO LATE.

Wendy Nather, Research Director, Enterprise Security Practice at 451 Research, notes that the best cakes/companies have sugar/security baked in. "The typical reaction to missing security is to try to slap it on afterwards in the form of 'icing' (e.g., 'Can't we just put a firewall in front of it?')," noted Nather who believes that there are many security products that follow the "icing" model, such as web application firewalls. "It just isn't the same as baking the security in to begin with," said Nather. "It doesn't take a malicious hacker to break 'top of the cake' security", said Nather who noted, "My kids are very good at separating the icing from the cake."

———

Codebook—Either a collection of code terms or a book used to encode and decode messages (non-symbolic obfuscation).

Code-names—Name concealments for a person or object/item etc.

Code-text—The result of encoding a given communication (the plaintext). Similar to cipher-text, code-text differs mainly in that a code, rather than a cipher, conceals the text. **Code-numbers**—Function like codewords when they replace the words of a plaintext message. **Code-words**—see page 67.

———

<u>Forever</u> Is A Very Long Time!

Unfortunately, even a single hacked entry-method or exploited attack-surface—can lead to a data-breach that effectively invalidates all the other protective mechanisms. An attacker has to be successful just once (in relation to any number of attacks); whereas a defender must successfully protect datum(s) for each and every attack, or maintain a 100 percent success rate—forever!

Mega-Bug (first worldwide exploit example)

Glibc: Mega-bug That Threatens Thousands of Devices: A major CVE computer security vulnerability has been discovered—with experts cautiously warning it could potentially affect hundreds of thousands of devices, apps and services. However, due to the nature of the bug, it is extremely difficult to know how serious the problem is. "Many people are running around right now trying to work out if this is truly catastrophic or whether we have dodged a bullet," said Prof Alan Woodward, a security expert from the University of Surrey. Google engineers, working with security engineers at Red Hat, have released a patch to fix the problem. It is now up to manufacturers, and the community behind the Linux operating system, to issue the patch to affected software and devices as soon as possible. In a blog post explaining the discovery, Google's team detailed how a flaw in some commonly-used code could be exploited in a way that allows remote access to a device—be it a computer, internet router, or other connected piece of equipment. The code can also be within many of the so-called "building blocks" of the web—programming languages such as PHP and Python are affected, as well as systems used when logging in to sites or accessing email.—BBC News (17th February 2016)

Storage and Transfer Media

Sometimes, in order to achieve a primary-network design that provides **Absolute Security**—it may prove advantageous—to disentangle/separate—**transfer** from **storage** functionality. Such an approach can reduce the number of attack-surfaces and/or copies (i.e central copies) that are exposed to attack—and thus render the probability of a successful data-breach far less likely (i.e by moving to a P2P network design). It is important to realise that **socially secure communication** does not (necessarily) include back-up function(s). **Single-copy-send** is not multiple-copy-send—and does not require the creation of central storage/backup-copies. For Absolute Security, it may be best to let the sender/receiver take care of any and all backup function(s) for themselves—and in terms of creating their own data/account backup(s)—locally (i.e on a PC)—and/or by means of organisational backups etc.

Public Communication Channel(s)

By definition, any and all data packets flowing along public communication channel(s)/pipeline(s)—existing on an open-network—or the Internet—**ARE—IN SOME ASPECT—PUBLIC.** This is because data-packets must be routed along public data channel(s)—and using known IP and/or HTTP protocols etc. Hence all private-datums, no matter how they are represented—pass along the public information-highway. Ergo, and patently, secure communication involves 'squashing' private datum-copies into public datagrams.

CHAPTER 9

Bigger Brain

Versus

Stealth Techniques

THE SUBJECT AT hand is the building of stealth defences—with respect to the safe transfer of meaning between individual human beings. Accordingly, we specify aspects of primary-network concealment; with a view to obtaining Absolute Security for communicated datum(s) [ref. Absolute Security: TARGET and METHOD(S)].[22]

A second goal of this chapter is to define and classify covert mechanism(s) for primary-network defence—by means of logically consistent definitions, analysis and exposition.

---

[22] The OED (2nd Edition) defines 'stealth' thusly: 1) The action or practice of stealing or taking secretly and wrongfully; theft. 2) Contrasted with force or violence. 3) The action of stealing or going furtively into or out of a place; the action of stealing or gliding along unperceived. 4) Furtive or underhand action, an act accomplished by eluding observation or discovery.

Evasion Attack(s)

In network security, *evasion* is bypassing network security in order to deliver an exploit, attack, or other form of malware to a target network or system, without detection [Axiom 56]. The security systems are rendered ineffective against well-designed evasion techniques, in the same way that a stealth fighter can attack without detection by radar.

Stealth Defence(s)

A nice antipodal proposition—and remedy for—an evasive attack—is a *stealth defence*. Whereby all physical and virtual system gateways are rendered invisible and/or out-of-reach of the data-processing actions of any harmful attackers [Axiom 57].

Gateway Protection

A good rule-of-thumb for achieving—socially secure communication—is that it is always easier (and more effective) to eliminate/conceal a system gateway than to protect access to the same gateway [Axiom 58]. Ergo Absolute Security involves excluding/disguising entry-point(s) and entry-method(s) for unsafe-actors on the primary-network's data-processing stack.

A **system gateway** provides a way to access private datum-copies that exist on the primary-network's data-processing stack (legitimate entry or not). A gateway provides an access pathway for a copy—potentially bypassing any unrelated entry-defences that may exist for the system as a whole.

———

Countermeasure—By definition, a **defence-method** (or a **Countermeasure**) is a mechanism that prevents unauthorised parties (i.e. unsafe-actors) from gaining entry to one or more system gateway(s). Patently, the designer wishes to minimise the chances of a data-breach—and he/she does so by: A) protecting gateways; and B) reducing gateway: A) numbers, B) potential access location(s), C) time/exposure windows, and D) entry pathway types/numbers.

In the present chapter we are concerned with how best to protect form based attack-surface(s); consisting of **physical-gateways**—media of storage, transfer and access; and **virtual-gateways**—formatted copies for storage, transfer and access.

Patently—a wide range of—defensive techniques are possible—to protect gateway type(s); and because systems of communication are many and varied. Ergo, it is difficult to identify any universally applicable defensive procedures—without precedence.

Nevertheless, we can outline key principles for *primary-network concealment*—the same being methods that may prove useful to the designer of a system that seeks to provide Absolute Security.

Effective—STEALTH TECHNIQUES [Axiom 59]—

—include (for defence):

BLOCK

Move access-node(s)—plus related data-set(s)—including user data (i.e. user owned IDs/keys)—to a private (possibly portable) access-device; closing physical/virtual gateway(s).

RESTRICT

Employ an invitation-only-network + cypher-matching— whereby unsafe parties are blocked (i.e use a private network).

list continues overleaf...

DECEPTION

Use false/null data-traffic, decoys, honey-pots, spoofed access-device IP/MAC addresses (hide source + destination IDs/point(s)); hide message(s) in innocuous content; closing invalid gateway(s).

SECRECY

Use a secret/scrambled/coded protocol (key-protected); secret routers/gateways—to close/protect all datum physical/virtual-gateway(s).

CURTAIL

Eliminate all legitimate and illegitimate secondary copies (e.g. use a Peer-to-Peer (P2P) network); closing physical + virtual gateway(s).

DEFEND

Protect the communication channel (e.g. use distributed transport and/or concealed packet(s)).

CONCEAL

Conceal the method(s) of coding within a large range of possible method(s) + vary/overlap method(s); that is protect meaning gateway(s) (i.e. exploit the beholder's share).

LOCALISE

Localise Identity and Access Management System(s). Do not trust private items to nth-parties.

CONFUSE

Employ nested protective layers (ref. physical/virtual gateways).

———

In a nutshell, we wish to reduce gateway: exposure (limit existence in place/time), number(s), visibility and fragility—eliminating/nullifying attack-vectors [Axiom 60].

The title of the present chapter—*Bigger Brain versus Stealth Techniques'*—refers to what we regard as best-practice for building an—absolutely secure—point-to-point system for private communication of meaning. Put simply, we believe that it is far better to rely on stealth techniques—in order to *block/eliminate/conceal* system gateway(s)—than attempt to have a **bigger brain** than all attackers (i.e use ***unbreakable locks***).

Remember that for a central-server network; the primary, secondary, tertiary copies etc; hang around effectively <u>forever</u>—and are backed-up repeatedly. Undertaking to build an unbreakable encryption defence and/or coding method for such (effectively immortal) copies; may be unrealistic.

Ergo, attaining robust meaning gateway(s)—is predicated upon—maintenance of superior intelligence /know-how (perpetually)—and because the defence mechanism(s) must stay (at least) one step ahead of all attacker(s)—now and at all times in the future.

A preferable approach—and one that will prove to be—in all likelihood—far less vulnerable to a data-breach; is to move system gateways—beyond the reach of any attackers. Primary-network concealment can be achieved using fundamental techniques that do not rely on having a bigger brain (so-to-speak). Rather we employ carefully chosen hardware and software tools as described—for example—in the list above.

Gateway Architecture

As previously defined, an **access-gateway** consists of one or more access-nodes and/or (potentially) exposed attack-surfaces for a primary, secondary or tertiary copy. Earlier in Chapter 7 we characterised three different types of access-gateway for datum-copies existing on a point-to-point communication system.

Firstly, we have **physical-gateway(s)**—which determine who may obtain a physical copy; next we have **virtual-gateway(s)**—which determine who can open a virtual/formatted copy; and finally we have **meaning-gateway(s)** that determine who can decode a copy. To be successful an intruder must (typically) pass through several (nested) physical and virtual gateway(s); before decoding all meaning gateway(s)—and in order to uncover the communicated datum(s) [Axiom 61]. Ergo gateway defence-method(s) and/or entry-barriers—typically provide a hierarchy of defensive 'high-walls'—much like a castle (**defence-in-depth**).

Obviously, for Absolute Security [ref. Absolute Security: TARGET + METHOD(S)], it is best to employ as many nested gateway defences as possible—and in order to maximise the number and depth of defensive mechanism(s) present. However, as stated, it is normally best practice to render (as many as possible) access-gateways—invisible and/or out-of-reach for unwarranted actor(s). Ergo, primary-network entry-method blocking/concealment would seem to be the best approach for defending a communication pipeline; combined with elimination of any unnecessary secondary copies—plus protection of potential tertiary copies.

Short Timescales—A nice stealth defensive mechanism is to limit attack-surface exposure(s) to very short timescales—providing only fleeting visibility to unsafe actors. For example sending datum-copies from one portable USB key-drive to another, whilst using a P2P network (i.e. limited access-node exposure and no central copy exposure).

We can conclude that the techniques of Absolute Security are not rocket science—but they are a little unusual in that they do require specialist tools; including potentially: *Peer-to-Peer (P2P) network design, stealth and depth-defences, well-designed encryption/coding, plus localised—or P2P—user ID/key management system(s), user-owned passwords, secret-keys etc.*

Let us now go back to the original purpose of this book. Remember that we had made a distinction between partial/absent and Absolute Security [ref. Absolute Security: TARGET]. Perhaps for most situations it is fine to have a small degree of additional security provided by a standard encryption method (e.g. using email with a single-layer of encryption). But for those occasions when one has to communicate datum(s) that are of a particularly high value (i.e. be *private-by-guarantee*)— then we must employ special techniques.

Unfortunately, attaining Absolute Security is challenging using standard (central-server) tools such as email and file-sharing systems like **DropBox**, **GoogleDrive** etc; because— as we have seen—these systems are potentially open to a host of exploits, intercepts and data-breaches.

Such problems relate to structural vulnerabilities in terms of network design (i.e. long-term exposure of physical gateways); leaving only virtual and meaning gateway protective techniques.

"The methods that will most effectively minimize the ability of intruders to compromise information security are comprehensive user training and education. Enacting policies and procedures simply won't suffice. Even with oversight the policies and procedures may not be effective: my access to Motorola, Nokia, ATT, Sun depended upon the willingness of people to bypass policies and procedures that were in place for years before I compromised them successfully" — Kevin Mitnick

Private by Guarantee

Privacy can be defined as **socially restricted access** for an item, and it is a status that must be upheld/defended by some protective methods (i.e specific accessibility pathways in terms of who may see, know and/or change the item).

Private-by-guarantee means that there is no possibility of the item's privacy status being changed (by any unwarranted actor(s))—at any place/time—and under any circumstances whatsoever.

Feudal Security

With the prevalence of cloud services and locked-down user devices, we're entering a world where IT security is very reminiscent of feudalism. We pledge allegiance to companies like Apple or Google, and in return they promise to protect us. We have little or no control over the security of our iPad, or Gmail accounts, or Facebook data, or Flickr photos; we simply have to trust our feudal lords. Of course, these lords don't always have our best interests at heart, and can easily take advantage of us," said Bruce Schneier author of 'Liars and Outliers'.

Semagram

A form of steganography, wherein encryptions are made of arrangements of objects, images, or symbols rather than by letters or numbers.

Coded Transmission(s) versus Coded Meaning(s)

By definition, a datagram exists—on a networked system—in the form of a hierarchy of coded layers. Whereby the process of transferring a group of related datum-copies (for example letters in a text-file) from one IP node to another; requires that lower level binary bits are used to assemble higher level packetised structures—which in turn create individual ASCI letters. This is an example of **Coded Transmission(s)**—or the use of public codes to facilitate data transfer(s). Such code types are sharply distinguished from the **Coding of Meaning**—whereby secret codes are used to mask and/or conceal the meaning of communicated symbols—and by means of unusual symbol-meaning mapping(s) etc.

Zero Day Vulnerability—A zero day vulnerability refers to a hole in software that is unknown to the vendor. This security hole is then exploited by hackers before the vendor becomes aware and hurries to fix it—this exploit is called a **zero day attack.**

In summary, attaining *Absolute Security* for our digital communication(s)—is a *difficult-to-reach*—but not impossible goal. Just like the magician, rather than performing any real magic tricks (achieving unbreakable encryption/coding)—we misdirect.

Accordingly,

we seek to:

A. Lock/block/conceal system gateway(s);

B. Conceal the method(s) of entry/defence (variable aspects) within a large range—of (potential) methods;

C. Employ depth-defences to confuse/ slow-down an attacker.

In this manner (A+B+C) [named as Axiom 62],

we safeguard attack-surface entry-methods.

* * * * *

Shannon's Maxim

We consider that Shannon's maxim: 'assume the enemy knows the system' refers purely to aspects of an entry/defence-method's **form** <u>alone</u> (i.e conceptual form/design of the locking/blocking/concealing entry/defence mechanism(s)). Whereas aspects of the instantiation of the employed secure **entry/defence-method(s)** (i.e. secret-keys/coding variables and/or particular access-device location(s)/node-login-details)—may obviously remain secret.

And because this is what security is—protection of privacy by means of restricted/robust **entry/defence-method(s)**—system elements that cannot be fraudulently discovered/used/over-run; or defences that are inaccessible to unsafe-actors. However it may be that Shannon meant to say that a defender should avoid—relying upon secrecy by means of identical locking/blocking/concealing techniques (i.e the **same form(s)**)—over-and-over again—and because they may (or certainly will) be discovered. Ergo, one can still rely on secrecy of an **entry/defence-method's form**—if it **changes often enough**—and without (necessarily) compromising security in any way.

We posit that the well-known Shannon's/Kerckhoffs's principle has been misinterpreted to drive the security community away from deception (aka stealth-based security systems/mechanisms).

Use of term Secret

In footnote 22 (plus the note above), **secret** refers to a socially restricted entry-method that is known/usable only by the sender and receiver parties

The Cyber Ripple Theory

...states that "the effect of a cyber attack on an organisation or individual has a destructive cascading effect both on the connecting technology and the human aspects that are linked. Further the extend of the destruction depends on the awareness and protection levels around the sequential points of the attack."—Professor Richard Benham—May 2014

CHAPTER 10

Privacy And Security:

The Big Picture

THE SUBJECT AT hand is the safe transfer of meaning between individual human beings.

Accordingly, we specify key principles of design for a nominal primary-network; and with a view to obtaining Absolute Security for communicated datum(s)[ref. Absolute Security: TARGET)].

A second goal of this chapter is to define and classify safe mechanism(s) for primary-network defence—by means of logically consistent definitions, analysis and exposition.[23]

---

[23] In a nutshell, we can characterise a private/secure communication system as being concerned with: A) *locking/blocking/concealing: physical/virtual system access gateway(s)*; B) *Providing sufficiently secure Identity and Access Management mechanism(s)*—including properly secure secret-keys/unlocking mechanism(s)/logins & passwords etc; and: C) *Protecting—or locking—meaning gateways* by means of sufficiently robust encryption and coding mechanism(s).

Over the past nine chapters, we have developed a new top-level theory of secure point-to-point system(s) for private communication of meaning. Along the way, we identified—a logically consistent—set of terms, principles and recommendations; with which to characterise and compare-and-contrast the different security system types. Largely, implementation details have been cast aside—but (hopefully) not at the expense of lucidity, rigour and/or truthful analysis.

Space limitations have precluded any—detailed analysis of—**Identity/Access/Secret-Key Management System(s)**—however these topics have been well-examined elsewhere—and in lower-level treatment(s). In any case, we are now in position to ask: what does an ideal system look like—what are its specific features—and how can we deliver Absolute Security?

Ofttimes manufacturers put forward the view that a particular networked system is immune to hacking/spying as a result of this fact—or for that pre-eminent reason—and/or simply because it uses that method etc.

But if there is a key lesson of the Cybersecurity field—it has been that no single defensive technique is a source of ultimate safety—rather it is the *whole system that must be secure, by design, implementation and operation.*

Today's systems must <u>anticipate</u> future attacks.

Any comprehensive system—whether for authenticated communications, secure data storage, or electronic commerce—is likely to remain in use for five years or more.

Consider also the lifetime(s) of any/all datum-copies!

The system (plus copy protections)—must be able to withstand the future. smarter attackers, more computational power, and greater incentives to subvert a widespread system. There won't be time to upgrade it in the field.

Patently, the designer does not (and cannot) know what will be the precise user-case scenario(s)—or specific nature(s) of the complex technological environment(s—in which a particular communication system will be used.

Hence what can be done?

In a nutshell, it is my belief that we must—fight for the right—to recognise, know and comprehend what are the underlying principles—plus assumptions—used in each case. Accordingly, we need an open, valid—all-encompassing— *theory of information security*—and primarily to define what it actually means (*logically*, *philosophically*, *technically* and *socially*) to keep information safe.

Ergo, and by means of this book, we henceforth submit a new (unified) theory of Absolute Security.[24]

* * * * *

---

[24] In his famous paper 'Communication Theory of Secrecy Systems', Dr Claude Shannon made a distinction between three types of **secrecy** as follows: A) **Concealment Systems**—in which the existence of the message is concealed from the enemy—or in our terms physical/virtual/meaning gateway concealment (finding action(s) are blocked); and B) **Privacy Systems**—which use special equipment to recover the message (i.e. transfer/access/storage—and (for example) physical/virtual gateway blocking (form entry pathway action(s) blocked)); and C) **'True' Secrecy Systems**—whereby the meaning of the message is concealed by cipher/code etc; (i.e. metrical, descriptive and selectional attack-surfaces are protected (content entry action(s) are locked)).

In his paper Shannon explored (rigorously) only the 3rd secrecy type—whereas in this short book we have—at least superficially—analysed all three types. Ergo, we have identified three different gateways types—physical/virtual/meaning; plus three classes of attack surface(s) that may exist within a specific meaning gateway.

Skepticism

It is prudent to apply skepticism in response to any forthright claims of impregnability when it comes to a (standardised) digital communication system. In light of recent events (NSA spying & Edward Snowden etc), it has become clear that conventional systems are far less secure than most people had realised. Ergo, we can no longer listen to the security promises/guarantees of some rather narrow Cybersecurity 'experts'—without a certain degree of scepticism; and because countless data-breaches indicate that (at least some) people were either lying, deceptive or just plain wrong.

Accordingly, we need to know what has gone wrong with security systems—on a world-wide basis—because everyday we see new instances of stolen, lost and compromised data—and on systems that were supposed to be impregnable. We need a new open language of security vulnerability, plus assessment methods to judge one system against another. We might also ask—who is designing our technologies—and why? Have we been lied-to/deceived? If so, what can we do about it—and how?

Incredibly, some security 'experts' do not ever connect their personal computers to the Internet! It is as if they had given up—and believe that nothing (no security defence) offered even the slightest chance of protection. Most people are not so lucky as the same 'experts' who can simply disconnect from the Internet—and then run around giving everyone else (somewhat contradictory) advice.

Brute Force Hacking

Brute Force is a cryptanalysis technique or other kind of attack method involving an exhaustive procedure that tries all possibilities, one-by-one.

Information Security Indicators

Benchmarking of computer security requires measurements for comparing both different IT systems and single IT systems. The technical approach is a pre-defined catalog of security events (security incident and vulnerability (computing)) together with corresponding formula for the calculation of security indicators that are accepted and comprehensive.

Information Security Indicators have been standardised by the ETSI Industrial Specification Group (ISG) ISI. These indicators provide the basis to switch from a qualitative to a quantitative culture in IT Security Scope of measurements: External and internal threats (attempt and success), user's deviant behaviours, nonconformities and/or vulnerabilities (software, configuration, behavioural, general security framework).

The European Telecommunications Standards Institute (ETSI) is an independent, not-for-profit, standardisation organisation in the telecommunications industry.

Money, Time and Resources

The problem most organisations will have with proper security is that it is complex to administer, can be hard to use, expensive and typically requires specialised, disciplined people and tech. Security policy must also be valued and adhered to by the rest of the organisation's stakeholders.

Figure 8 & 9: Circular Security: Meaning Gateway(s)

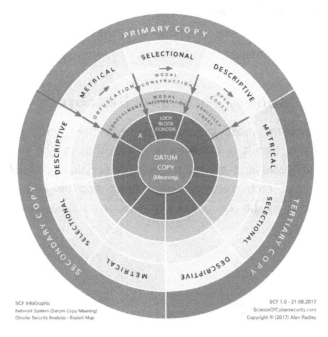

THE BIG PICTURE

Figure 10 & 11: Circular Security: Form Gateway(s)

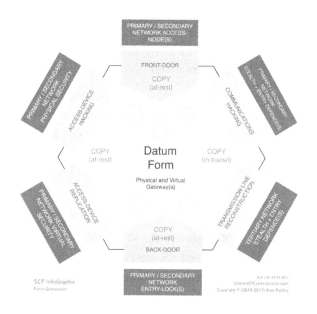

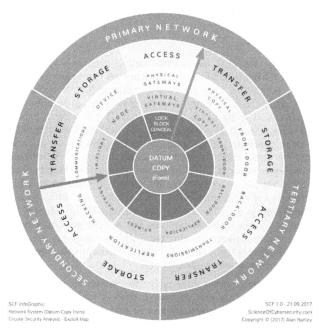

Theory / Logic / System

Theory: A conception or mental scheme of something to be done, or of the method of doing it; a systematic statement of rules or principles to be followed.

Logic: The branch of philosophy concerned with the use and study of valid reasoning. Among the important properties of logical systems are: *consistency* (no contradictory theorems), *validity* (no false inferences), *completeness* (true and provable formulae), and *soundness* (premises are true in the actual world).

System: A set or assemblage of things connected, associated, or interdependent, so as to form a complex unity; a whole composed of parts in orderly arrangement according to some scheme or plan.

Theory of Absolute Security: A logical scheme and/or prescribed system for providing socially secure communication.[25]

---

[25] How might we best summarise and/or develop—optimistically—a philosophy of **Absolute Security**? Perhaps we can begin by stating that: A) for two parties to communicate a message (i.e. datum(s)) privately and with guaranteed security; and by means of: B) a communication channel that is in some sense 'public'; then C) it is a basic premise that the two parties must (by some method) protect (lock/block/conceal) the message content(s) from access by other (unwarranted) parties; and D) that the protection is performed by means of **wholly/partially secret entry-method(s)** (including the locking/blocking/concealing of accessibility action(s))—which enables only legitimate parties to unlock the communicated meaning; whereby: E) the **protected entry-method(s)** must remain (at least partially) private (in terms of form and/or content); and F) typically the **protected entry-method(s)** consist of some private locking/blocking/concealment: mechanism(s)/ key(s)/algorithm(s)/physical-device(s)/transmission-protocol(s)/ entry-paths/interpretive-method(s) etc.

N.B. Ultimately, **there is no alternative** to the holding (by both parties— or sender/receiver)—of one-or-more—shared **wholly secret entry-method(s)** and/or **partially secret entry-method(s)**.

Information-Security Crisis

It is interesting to note that a good deal of disagreement exists amongst the experts—as to which point-to-point communication system, if any, is fully secure. For example, practitioners have long argued over symmetric (local private shared key) and asymmetric (PGP) encryption—with proponents from both sides claiming that the other's methods are inherently are more vulnerable. What we can say with certainty is that neither side is correct—and that both methods have drawbacks—depending upon the specific features of a particular user-case scenario.

According to recent press revelations, a variety of back-doors have been built into standard encryption methods.

For example, random number generators have been deliberately altered to make them—less than random. Ergo, all dependent ciphers are rendered somewhat less than secure (regardless of user passwords etc).

It is now commonplace to hear of numerous other systematic data-breaches and encryption-related problems (i.e. deliberate and/or accidental vulnerabilities). It is obvious that the information-security field is in crisis.

Accordingly, we must now *re-evaluate the entire field of information-security*—and re-examine its founding principles and core assumptions. At the same time, we must impel system designers to work on more effective solutions for information-security. We put a man on the moon—surely it is not beyond the ken of humans to make secure and private communication a viable option—and for everyone/anytime.

Cyberwarfare specialists cautioned this week that the Internet was effectively a "wilderness of mirrors," and that attributing the source of cyberattacks and other kinds of exploitation is difficult at best and sometimes impossible. Despite the initial assertions and rumors that North Korea was behind the attacks and slight evidence that the programmer had some familiarity with South Korean software, the consensus of most computer security specialists is that the attackers could be located anywhere in the world.

— John Markoff

It used to be expensive to make things public and cheap to make them private. Now it's expensive to make things private and cheap to make them public.

— Clay Shirky

We have built as a government something called the National Cyber Investigative Joint Task Force, NCIJTF, where 19 federal agencies sit together and divide up the work. See the threat, see the challenge, divide it up and share information.

— James Comey

CHAPTER 11

A Theory of

Absolute Security

OUR GOAL has been to characterise a communication system for replicating information patterns—encapsulated as discrete units of data (messages/files/folders)—between remote computer nodes; whilst preserving the social integrity (privacy) of said patterns in place and time.

A second goal was to define safe mechanism(s) for primary-network defence—by means of logically consistent definitions, analysis and exposition.

Overall, and along-the-way—we have specified a new theory of **Absolute Security.** This same theory provides a unified set of concepts and first-principles; and hence design guidelines—with which to define/provide: *socially secure communication.* Accordingly, I leave it to the reader to appraise the extent to which the aforementioned goals have been met; and to adjudge the validity/usefulness of the proposed—theory of Absolute Security.

In the OED, **Absolute** is define thusly: 1) Detached, disengaged, unfettered. 2) Absolved, loosened, detached, disengaged (from). 3a) Disengaged from all accidental or special circumstances; essential, general. 3b) Absolute in quality or degree; perfect. 4a) Free from all imperfection or deficiency; complete, finished; perfect, consummate. 4b) Originally: absolved, disengaged: then adj. disengaged or free from imperfection or qualification; from interference, connexion, relation, comparison, dependence; from condition etc.

Doubtless, it is a truism that sometimes one cannot see the *wood-for-the-trees* in terms of identifying the precise relationships between the technical (structural) aspects of how a system works and its varied—and perhaps unpredictable (functional) influences on the wider human/social world.

A blindspot may exist in terms of understanding how a system operates to produce certain functional outcomes.

Sometimes (or often) we do not have a full understanding of how—or why—a system works structurally; and due to factors such as the *diversity*, *complexity* and the *partial invisibility* of operational situation(s), plus due to the presence of hidden/ unpredictable influencing factors and/or unknown/ arbitrary low-level design features etc.

But if any blindspot(s) also exist for the designers/ operators, then it may be that we are all in very serious trouble, because it would appear that nobody knows—or can begin to explain—what may be the functional effect(s) of our systems, computers and machines.

Accordingly, we (the users) must be able to understand (at the very least) what are the operating principles/assumptions for our communication technologies; and in particular *how*, *when*, *where* and *why*; they interrelate with wider *social workflows* to form everyday communication systems.

But in terms of present-day systems, this is precisely what we often do <u>not</u> have—knowledge of the ways in which our systems may (possibly) fail to live up to our expectations in the future (ref. forever is a very long time!).

In other words—in this book—we uphold open-security—not-so-much in terms of specific security method(s)—but rather for top-level design principle(s).

It has been our position that for—information-security —missing are **axiomatic principles/laws**—or founding definitions/propositions related to the 'human-side' of the equation. Consequently, we have endeavoured to bring *truth, unity, clarity* and *logical structure*—or holism—to the topic of socially secure communication.

I need hardly remind the reader of the very real problem(s) facing anyone who wished to obtain certainty in relation to protecting the privacy of his/her digital communications. Many people believe that **Absolute Security** is, quite simply, impossible to achieve.

Why should this be the case? And why is there a widespread belief that—it is somehow inevitable—that current systems must be fundamentally insecure?

Patently, the answer relates (partly) to the countless data-breaches that occur on a daily basis. And astoundingly, it seems that the very same people who advised us on Cybersecurity—the world's top experts—have actually helped the **NSA** build encryption back-doors into vast numbers of *computers, phones* and *networked devices*.

Unfortunately however, these same back-door(s) are available to hackers. Nevertheless, perhaps the NSA have done us all a favour—by (inadvertently) exposing an industry—information-security—that is rampant with false-promises and undelivered guarantees.

Professor Phillip Rogaway has recently written an article entitled *'The Moral Failure of Computer Scientists'*— and in relation to this specific issue (2016).

Identity Authentication

Two Factor Authentication, also known as 2FA, two step verification or TFA (as an acronym), is an extra layer of security that is known as **"multi factor authentication"** that requires not only a password and username but also something that only the user has on them, i.e. a (second) piece of information that only they possess. Often 2FA/TFA can usefully employ something only the user can physically display (e.g. finger-prints, retina pattern)— in order to enhance security protection.

Password Entry Systems employ a **password**—which is a word or string of characters used for user authentication to prove identity or access approval to gain access to a resource (example: an access code is a type of password), which should be kept secret from those not allowed access. Despite the name, there is no need for passwords to be actual words; indeed passwords which are not actual words may be harder to guess, a desirable property. The terms **passcode** and **passkey** are sometimes used when the secret information is purely numeric, such as the personal identification number (PIN) commonly used for ATM access.

British Standard 7799: A standard code of practice and provides guidance on how to secure an information system. It includes the management framework, objectives, and control requirements for information security management systems.

Password-Strength—A concise work on 'password-strength' has been given in:

'A Canonical Password Strength Measure'
—by Eugene Panferov (http://arxiv.org/abs/1505.05090)

———

Abuse(s) of Power: In his book 'The Future of Human Rights', human ethics Professor Upendra Baxi, says that human rights languages, however effete remain perhaps all that we have to interrogate the barbarism of power. Baxi says: human rights are the best hope there is for a participative making, and re-making of human futures.

What can be done to bring belief/trustworthiness—back to the field of information-security?

Perhaps we can begin by asking: what is the nature of private communication? In this respect—we offer up a quick hint—by suggesting that privacy and security (for interpersonal communication(s))—may be fundamental human right(s). I know that related issue(s) are contentious—and much debated—but surely we (as a people) should at least consider the implications of the **United Nations Declaration of Human Rights**—with respect to the free exchange of ideas (i.e. protection of open/private/secret thoughts).

We might even consider creating an *Information-Security Declaration of Human Rights (or techno-rights)*—in terms of the provision of founding principles—for computer, system and machine design(s).

Placing such (utopian?) ideas aside, we must acknowledge that networked communication system(s) exist in a dangerous—and unlawful—environment that is analogous to the American Old or Wild-West.

Whereby countless unsafe-actors represent real danger(s) to communicated private-datum(s).

What to do?

Well firstly, we need full disclosure/agreement—and in relation to valid **founding principles** for the field of Cybersecurity (plus related: *axioms, definitions, logics, designs and policies* etc)—and in order to be able to build truly effective communication tools. Evidently, it is necessary to bring the computer back to an original purpose—interpersonal communication without spies/hacks/data-breaches.

Breaking Encryption

Breaking encryption with brute force is all about time and resources. The more time and resources an attacker must devote to their attack, the harder it is for them to succeed.

The added "strength" of two layers is that it is already difficult to break one layer of encryption, so breaking two layers will be even more difficult. Remember that encryption is just one (important) link in the security chain. If we apply the "inner fortress" principle, the very hardest encryption or defence layers will be on the inside. The assumption is that attackers are more easily detected (or worn out) as they attempt to penetrate increasingly difficult security perimeters. Medieval castles were built on similar principles as are most secure installations. First the moats, pikes and outer walls, then the hot pitch and finally the fortified, elevated keep.

Purpose of Private Thoughts

On the existence and need for secret and private-thoughts/ideas/datum(s): Why do we have thoughts in any case; fundamentally because they are for personal and private use; what is the alternative—automatons who are told what to think, say and do?

Conceal by Decoy: Another way to mask an item's structure is by hiding real content (or meaning) within a layer of apparently ordinary/innocuous content—wherein (for example) you sign off a message with 'Sincerely Yours'—whenever you agree with the message contents, or just 'Regards'—when you do not agree etc.

On-Premise versus Cloud Storage: A pressing concern for many is the extra operational challenge of on-premise data storage. To ease the pain, Iron Mountain recommends a tiered information storage approach that defines what is most used, most critical and most confidential, as well as what is dormant, and structuring storage, access and backup accordingly.

In summary, we must impel designers to work on more effective solutions when it comes to information-security; using rational/ethical principles based on logically consistent—and publicly visible/critique-able—definitions, axioms, concepts and theories.

Ergo, my hope is that—the *Theory of Absolute Security*—introduced here—can prove useful for application to future point-to-point system(s) for private communication of meaning.

*****

Noteworthy Issues / Questions

- Key protection is a classic case of 'who guards the guards?' It is possible to build key management processes around the idea of a quorum so that more than one administrator is needed to administer keys. Alternatively, you could use local key storage—and remove all n-th parties from the risk register.

- You have to ask yourself two questions: first, is there any chance that we can be more secure than a company that specialises in technology and knows that information security is core to its very existence? And second, who would really give a damn about what we hold on our disks anyway?

- And best practice security procedures, process and constant vigilance are equally vital, because the security boundaries, vulnerabilities and goal posts will always be shifting. If you don't keep repairing and fortifying the castle walls or fail to keep an eye out for the latest marauders, eventually you will fall.

- Breaking encryption with brute force is all about time and resources. The more time and resources an attacker must devote to their attack, the harder it is for them to succeed. The added "strength" of two layers is that it is already difficult to break one layer of encryption, so breaking two layers will be even more difficult. Remember that encryption is just one (important) link in the security chain. If we apply the "inner fortress" principle, the very hardest encryption or defence layers will be on the inside. The assumption is that attackers are more easily detected (or worn out) as they attempt to penetrate increasingly difficult security perimeters. Medieval castles were built on similar principles as are most secure installations. First the moats, pikes and outer walls, then the hot pitch and finally the fortified, elevated keep.

"Criminals and states that want to attack organisations can now choose from vast catalogues of pre-made malware", an expert explained, meaning that although the number of attacks is not increasing, they are becoming increasingly sophisticated. "The provision of malware is now big business," another explained. "It comes with the same kind of guarantees that software from Microsoft or one of the other big software houses has."

Business Reporter
— 2015 Cyber-Security Summary

Christian Toon, previous head of information risk in Europe for Iron Mountain, (now with PwC) believes companies should "Capture the generation, distribution, accounting, storage, use and destruction of cryptographic keying material and issue a high-level key management policy to guide the business users," he says.

VPNs, Private and Public Networks

A **virtual private network (VPN)** extends a **Private Network** across a public network, and enables users to send and receive data across shared or public networks as if their computing devices were directly connected to the private network. Applications running across the VPN may therefore benefit from the functionality, security, and management of the private network.

In the Internet addressing architecture, a **private network** is a network that uses private IP address space, following the standards set by RFC 1918 for Internet Protocol Version 4 (IPv4), and RFC 4193 for Internet Protocol Version 6 (IPv6). These addresses are commonly used for home, office, and enterprise local area networks (LANs).

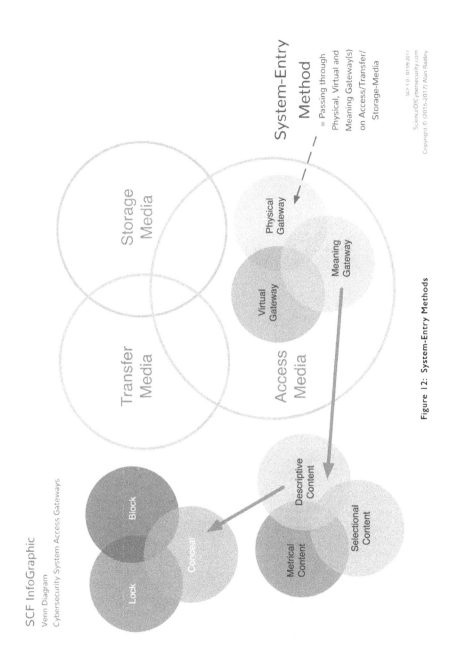

SCF InfoGraphic
Venn Diagram
Cybersecurity System Access Gateways

Storage Media

Transfer Media

Access Media

Physical Gateway

Virtual Gateway

Meaning Gateway

Descriptive Content

Selectional Content

Metrical Content

Conceal

Block

Lock

System-Entry Method

= Passing through Physical, Virtual and Meaning Gateway(s) on Access/Transfer/ Storage-Media

SCF 1.0 07.09.2017
ScienceOfCybersecurity.com
Copyright © (2015–2017) Alan Radley

Figure 12: System-Entry Methods

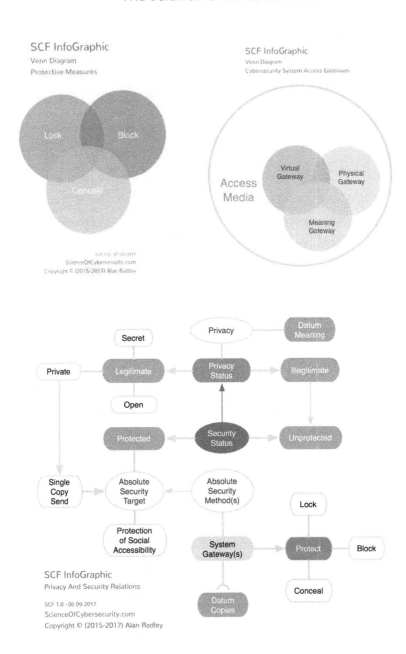

SCF InfoGraphic
Venn Diagram
Protective Measures

SCF InfoGraphic
Venn Diagram
Cybersecurity System Access Gateways

SCF InfoGraphic
Privacy And Security Relations

SCF 1.0 - 06.09.2017
ScienceOfCybersecurity.com
Copyright © (2015-2017) Alan Radley

Figure 13: Privacy And Security Relations

CHAPTER 12

Real Life Scenarios

AS WE bring this treaties on *The Science of Cybersecurity* to a close; it is appropriate to reflect on our findings. That is, to examine—or match—prescribed-theory with real-world security concerns.

Earlier we defined Absolute Security as *socially secure communication*—or *single-copy-send*—for a private-datum; in terms of safely transferring datum(s) from sender to receiver. We adopted a duel 'zoomed-in' plus 'wide-angled' perspective on privacy. Along the way we have— carefully mapped—key characteristics of privacy/ security—and (hopefully) by means of logical, scientific and insightful analysis—plus suitable terminology for attendant processes. Q.E.D.

But where are we now? Theory is—all very well and good—but it must have purpose. Unfortunately, several questions remain; such as: A) *what precisely is Absolute Security (in real-world terms); and B) how is it obtained; and even C) can it be obtained.*

Cyberwarfare—More and more, modern warfare will be about people sitting in bunkers in front of computer screens, whether remotely piloted aircraft or cyber weapons.—Philip Hammond

Earlier we pinned down *Absolute Security* thusly...

Absolute Security—for a point-to-point communication system—is the replication of a single instance (or *primary-copy*) of a datum from one socially restricted access-node to another [ref. Absolute Security: TARGET].

In other words, it is the *single-copy-send* of a datum from one party to another; whereby no—socially accessible—nth-party copies exist whatsoever (hopefully persistently)... thus—**ABSOLUTE SECURITY** and **PARTIAL/ ABSENT SECURITY**—are binary dualisms—or mutually exclusive true/false values for any act of communication.

Absolute security is protection of **privacy-status** for a datum-copy. Ergo, it relates to the maintenance of social accessibility restriction(s) for private-datum(s).

Whereby we achieve single-copy-send—now and (hopefully) at all times in the future. Accordingly, Absolute Security can be thought of as an objective true/false value, in and of itself. Hence an item either: *is absolutely secure*—or else: *it is not absolutely secure*— at any specific epoch—and for a particular environment /communication instance.

As stated, the Absolute Security TARGET is defined as single-copy-send for the encapsulated meaning (i.e certainty of protection). But it may be that at some post-communication epoch: A) the system/data is successfully hacked—and datum(s) are exposed to unsafe-actors; and hence B) the judgement of secure communication was/is/will-become false.

Consequently, privacy status may change; and security is patently a situation-specific/time-dependant quality.

As a result, it seems clear that Absolute Security must be—in one sense—a purely **objective property**. However because it is influenced by perceptions/judgements/predictions—it is at the same time a **subjective property**.

Evidently, factors such as: *inadequate knowledge of any/all unsafe-actors; plus hidden and changing threat types* —can cause incorrect and/or revised predictions in this respect. Henceforth making judgment(s)—as to the various *capability*, *coverage* and *control* aspects of security is especially difficult—because these are inevitably human assessed factors (automatic monitoring/reporting systems aside).

Absolute security status is simultaneously a *goal, metric, judgment and prediction;* in addition to being a real-world fact/truth. Accordingly, many interrelating factors are evident for a particular system operating at any specific epoch.

At the very least—the person making the Cybersecurity judgment(s)/decision(s) seeks to:

A. Be in possession of all the facts—or make accurate predictions on real-world: threats/defensive capabilities, and judge the effectiveness of threat-models; plus accuracy of monitoring system(s) etc; and

B. Adequately perceive/understand labyrinthine relationship(s) between multiple, complex, fixed and/or changing factors for relevant: systems/tools/networks/actors/attackers etc—including future ones; and

C. Implement valid Cybersecurity measures, plus avoid/correct mistakes etc.

The defender seeks to accurately: *perceive, measure and understand* all relevant factors; and so to assess which ones will influence overall Cybersecurity strategy. Ergo privacy status may be partly a *perception, model, prediction, belief* and/or *truth/falsehood*; depending upon your point of view and information/knowledge level(s).

Ultimately Cybersecurity involves assimilation of intelligence from as many as possible of the different: *threats, actors, systems, entry and defensive methods present.*

Hence Cybersecurity is an interdependent capability— and it must be constantly monitored and defended; plus—be (ideally) ever adapting to the changing needs/requirements of the open-network's perilous environment.

Unfortunately, the real-life situation may be even worse than this, because whenever you share access to a digital item—you trust: A) any and all primary/ secondary network users (i.e. *multiple humans*); plus; B) the communication-system itself (i.e. primary and secondary network security). Ergo, dangers may include both human and systematic vulnerabilities.

Earlier, we defined unauthorised datum-copy access (generally)—as an ordered series of goals—or a path—to be navigated. In real-world terms—any attacker desires the capability to *see/touch/open* a datum-copy's form and/or content. Attendant accessibility actions are *finding, contacting* and *knowing* a datum's meaning. Q.E.D.

Evidently, protecting any item from unsafe-actors— involves first building a defensive wall and/or unbridgeable barrier around it; prior to then providing an entrance-way for authorised parties (which must also be defended).

Whereby, the *finding action* (for a human/ programmatic actor and his/her helper actors) is detection of an item's material self (i.e. the datum-copy's form). For example, locating a datum-copy's form existing on a primary, secondary or tertiary network (media of access, storage and/or transfer for a copy).

Concordantly, the *contacting action* refers to the full mapping of datum-copy's interior form (true possession of content). Finally, the *knowing action* is the opening-up/ reading of meaning for the copy.

Accordingly, protecting access for unsafe-actors normally involves: *concealing* (ref. find); *blocking* (ref. contacting); and/or *locking* (ref. knowing); for datum-copies on the data-processing stack.

Henceforth this book has been concerned with techniques to afford protective measures for datum-copies.

Unfortunately measuring/quantifying the effectiveness—of any and all of these protective factors— may also be seen as judgments/predictions—in and of themselves. This is because they are (likewise) human-made/fallible entities that must cope with other (perhaps unknown) entities; specifically ones that may have been designed to nullify said anti-discovery/defensive techniques. Potentially present also (in the future) are multiple **human antagonists** who work to sweep-aside any security measures that are put in place.

What to do—and how/by-which-means?

Feasibly we can apply a little—deeper theory—and ask what is the nature of protection—or what are the most effective defensive techniques? (i.e. risk-free ones)

We begin with *concealment techniques.*

Evidently there are any number of different types of *concealment defences*—depending upon the specific nature of the entry-method/defence-method one is trying to conceal. For example, we can conceal existence by *masking structure* (in form, location and/or time).

Whereby there are three basic processes: A) *conceal by transformation* of form/location/time; or B) *conceal by similarity (equivalency)*—that is by hiding an item alongside a large number (of ostensibly identical) items; and C) *conceal by difference (complexity)*—or hiding an item amongst a large number of greatly/potentially varying forms/structures.

Fundamentally the process of masking detection—in this manner—requires just the right amount of concealment; and according to the specific capabilities of the penetration method(s) that are likely to be employed.

Likewise there are different types of *blocking techniques.*

We can block a system entrance pathway by eliminating it all-together (for a particular class of unsafe-actor); or else we can employ *navigation complexity and/or movement barriers* to make the path difficult to traverse. This can be achieved by filling the path with many *false-entrances,* or maze-like pathways etc. An example would be distributed data transport, and/or segmented transfer for datagrams.

Finally, it is feasible to *lock a system entrance gateway* by a means of special: *algorithm(s); watermark(s); facial, retina and finger-print recognition system(s) etc;* and/or other *diversity locks* (i.e. *secret patterns, methods, markers, keys etc*); combined with *content concealment* through transformation/similarity/difference.

And to top-it-all, defences can be overlaid—aka defence-in-depth or the **CASTLE** method. But perhaps we have gone about as far as a general theory can take us—in terms of making all-purpose recommendation(s) about how to protect copies existing on primary, secondary and tertiary networks. We simply do not know enough about the real-world systems/attack-methods in question. In any case, listing all of the potential attack/defence techniques used—would prove exhaustive.

By what means then, in a such a short book, can we summarise how the system designer/user should go about protecting a data-processing stack from all possible attacks?

The answer lies in asking and continually re-asking—the right questions—plus challenging assumptions—in relation to Cybersecurity.

Firstly, we desire to know—*what types of data require which types of protection and why—and for how long*. In the past (prior to Bradley Manning, the **Internet** etc); military organisations were very good at this type of thing—categorisation of security access levels etc. That is assigning confidentiality/accessibility levels to every item of data—or individual unit of information/knowledge.

However that was before open-network complexity exploded; and the attackers/attack-vectors multiplied in numbers, types, motivations and capabilities etc.

Nevertheless, a good rule-of-thumb—as detailed in Chapter 9—is to consider who needs to have access to the item/system and why. Physical and virtual denial/blocking techniques—to eliminate certain unsafe actors—may be the safest way to proceed.

Patently obvious—at the same time—is that we should involve all *partners, stakeholders, and legitimate users* in any Cybersecurity analysis or strategy development; plus operation(s). Everyone must be adequately briefed—continually—and on the changing nature of likely threats/responses.

When an individual must rely on his/her own capabilities—it becomes difficult to know where to go for advice. Do we trust the cloud providers like **Google** and **Apple**—or else look for P2P solutions; or even avoid/abandon the digital-world for our most private items?

Finding answers is not so easy—because they depend upon a host of technical, human and situation-specific factors.

It is often easier to make recommendations to people—in relation to Cybersecurity—who know a lot about the technical aspects of security; but less-so for less-technical people. This is so partly because less-geeky people (perhaps understandably) have other concerns, and/or they are not interested in all of the (confusing) technical details involved.

Here in this book we have avoided technical details—so far as we were able. The book has charted close-to-the-wind in terms of exploring relationships between a host of *technical and human-centric concepts/ principles* (hopefully to useful effect). Overall, we sought to unify the technical and human—opportunities and risks—for information security.

As stated—security is ***protection of privacy of meaning.***

However the simple logical clarity of this statement changes in certain subtle and difficult to determine ways—when it crosses-over into the realm of cyber.

In particular—in the digital-world—nothing is entirely private—and one must lock/block/conceal all illicit entry-methods for secret/private items. As many as possible of the *physical, virtual* and *meaning gateways* must be protected—and in order to retain any chance of achieving Absolute Security.

It is also my opinion, that attaining *Absolute Security*— or *assured protection*—in relation to the privacy of our interpersonal communication(s)—is not some impossible dream—mythical being—or paper-tiger. Rather, socially secure communication demands that the communicants abide by a relatively straight-forward set of principles and systemic/technological theory—and employ communication tools that do the same.

Nobody said it would be easy to *communicate privately, safely and with integrity plus assurance*; it isn't; but despite the existence of many dangers/pitfalls, *Absolute Security* is eminently achievable.[26, 27]

* * * * *

Privacy is not for the passive.

— Jeffrey Rosen

---

[26] **Information Security** is such a vastly complex—and rapidly evolving—technological field—that it is impossible to depict anything but a rudimentary facsimile (of a small sub-region) of the same in a single book. Nevertheless, holism is the key goal.

[27] **The Science of Cybersecurity** outlined here—whilst striving to be complete in terms of axioms, logic, founding principles and fundamental definitions etc; must (obviously) be seen as work in progress (for the security community as a whole).

Cybersecurity Lexicon

(Standard Terms Capitalized)

Absolute Security [TARGET]—for a point-to-point communication system—is the replication of a single instance (or primary-copy) of a datum—from one socially restricted access-node to another. In other words, it is the single-copy-send of a datum from one party to another; whereby no—socially accessible—nth-party copies exist whatsoever (hopefully persistently).

Absolute Security [METHOD(S)]—are continually working security: systems, rules, actors, networks, programs, defences and human/automatic operational procedures etc; that protect: An Absolute Security TARGET.

Access—Ability of an actor (or human) to see, know and/or change an item.

ACCESS CONTROL—Restricting access to resources to privileged entities.

Access-Device—Physical access device that enables a human to gain entry into a primary/secondary/tertiary network (i.e. a personal computer).

Access-Node—Virtual access gateway (login-node/ point-of-entry) for a primary/secondary/tertiary network.

ACCESS-MANAGEMENT—Protective methods for specific network access-node(s)—may involve management of User Identity, Secret Passwords etc—and the creation of protective techniques and armoured access-gateways for the system.

Access-Media—is a hardware/software system that enables an actor to see, know and/or change a copy's form and/or content.

Access-Gateway—consists of one or more access-nodes and/or exposed attack-surface(s)—for a primary, secondary or tertiary copy. The gateway is comprised of a group of hardware/software elements that together form an 'entrance aperture' for actor pathway(s). The gateway may be—open or shut—protected or unprotected—at any particular place/time—and for specific actor(s)/attack-vector(s)—and by means of access/locking mechanism(s).

Actor-Coherence (Defence)—is when all of the actors, entities and processes—present in a primary-network's data-processing stack—are impelled to act together in order to protect the private datum-copy's form and/or content from unwarranted social access (hopefully for all places/times).

Actor-Integrity—Unity of (data-processing) action (for all actors on the data-processing stack).

Actor Unity-of-Purpose—Unity of purpose and/or design (for all actors on the data-processing stack).

ALGORITHM—A series of instructions whereby a mathematical formula is applied to the numeric representation of a message in order to encrypt or decrypt it.

ATTACK-SURFACE—is an exposed facet/system entry-point for a datum-copy, existing on a primary-network's data-processing stack, and which (potentially) facilitates unwarranted social access to a private datum-copy's content and/or form.

ATTACK-VECTOR—is a specific data-processing path, existing on a primary-network's data-processing stack—which (potentially) provides unwarranted social access to a private datum-copy's content and/or form.

AUTHENTICATION—The process of verifying the sender or receiver as well as the contents of a communication. Conveyance, to another entity, of official sanction to do or be something.

BACK-DOOR—is an access-gateway provided by a primary-network vendor—that (possibly) enables one or more actors to bypass network security system(s) and obtain unauthorised access to private datum(s).

BEHOLDER'S SHARE—States that our perceptual experience—depends on the active interpretation of sensory input. Perception becomes a generative act, one in which biological and sociocultural influences conspire to shape the brain's 'best guess' of the causes (and meaning) of its sensory signals—or in our terms the meaning of the symbolic message being communicated. In the context of security systems—the Beholder's Share refers to methods for protecting meaning gateway(s) by means of secret/private modal contexts/interpretation(s) for communicated datum(s).

BINARY—having two components or possible states, usually represented by ones and zeros in varies patterns.

BIT—the smallest unit of information in a computer. Equivalent to a single zero or one.The word bit is a contraction of binary-digit.

CENTRAL-SERVER (Network)—Refers to cloud-server networks; such as email, Dropbox, Facebook, Twitter etc; in which all of the communicated data is relayed by—and stored on—centralised storage facilities.

CERTIFICATION—Endorsement of information by a trusted entity. CASTLE-DEFENCE—See Depth-Defence definition. CLOUD—See Central-Server definition.

CODE—(French, Latin: 'tree-trunk, 'writing tablet')—A method of concealment that may use words, numbers or syllables to replace original words/phrases of a message. Codes substitute whole words whereas ciphers transpose or substitute letters or digi-graphs. Also a disguised way of evoking meaning (non-symbolic obfuscation).

CODEBOOK—Either a collection of code terms or a book used to encode and decode messages.

CODE-NAMES—Name concealments for a person or object/item/datum etc.

Code-numbers—Numbers that function like codewords when they replace the words of a plaintext message.

CODE-TEXT—The result of encoding a given communication (the plaintext). Similar to cipher-text, code-text differs mainly in that a code, rather than a cipher, conceals the text.

Coding—is defined as the generation of descriptive and/or selectional layers for a representation.

Copy—Shorthand for Datum-Copy.

Content (Datum-Copy)—refers to the meaning content of a communicated datum. A representation (or datum) may have metrical, descriptive and selectional aspects—which work together to convey meaning.

COMMUNICATION (Human)—Transfer of discrete package(s) of meaning—messages—between people; or the one-to-one replication of datum(s) between minds + nominal meta-data (perhaps).

COUNTERMEASURE—Reactive methods used to prevent an exploit from successfully occurring once a threat has been detected. Intrusion Prevention Systems (IPS) commonly employ countermeasures to prevent intruders form gaining further access to a computer network. Other counter measures are patches, access control lists and malware filters.

CRYPTOGRAPHY—is defined as a secret manner of writing, either by arbitrary characters in other than the ordinary sense, or by methods intelligible only to those possessing a (private) key.

CYBER—Relating to the culture of computers, information technology, and virtual reality: the cyber age.

CYBER-ATTACK—An attempt by an unauthorised actor (person or computing agent)—to penetrate a digital system's security and gain unwarranted access to private/secret datum(s) contained therein.

CYBER-SECURITY—The state of being protected against criminal or unauthorised use of electronic data, or the measures taken to achieve this. Whereby all illegitimate actor(s) (i.e. unwarranted human plus machine actor(s), and their aid(s)/helper(s)) are prevented from **Accessing** (ie. Finding, Contacting and Knowing) a private/secret datum's **Form** and/or **Content**. Protection involves use of security protocols/mechanisms for **Locking**, **Blocking** and **Concealing** all system access gateways. In summary, Cybersecurity is the protection of social accessibility status for an item of meaning—or a Datum—and as such refers to the protection of **secrecy**, **privacy** or **openness** of meaning; or the safe transfer/storage/access of single/multiple Datum(s) between/for human(s).

CYBER-THREAT—-the possibility of a malicious attempt to damage or disrupt a computer network or system. Example usage: "the FBI has opened an investigation to address the potential cyberthreat".

CYPHER—a secret or disguised way of writing (symbolic obfuscation). Also a method of concealment in which the primary unit is the letter.

CIPHER ALPHABET—An alphabet composed of substitutes for the normal alphabet or the particular alphabet in which the cipher is written.

CLEAR TEXT—A communication sent without encoding or encryption. Such messages are also called in clear; or sometimes in plain language.

CRYPTOGRAM—An encoded or enciphered message.

Cypher-Matching—Security protocol for defending a network communication instance—whereby (prior to sending any private information/datum(s)) the sender access-node asks the receiver access-node to decrypt and answer a specific (secret) question—and in order to establish the identity of the receiver with a reasonable degree of confidence (coined by Alan Radley).

CYPHER-TEXT—In cryptography, cypher-text is the result of encryption performed on plaintext using an algorithm, called a cipher. The new enciphered communication is the cipher-text.

DATA INTEGRITY—Ensuring information has not been altered by unauthorized or unknown means.

Data-Processing Stack—the sum total of all the actors, entities and processes etc; existing on—and/or potentially influencing—a primary-network's communication 'pipeline'.

Datum—any idea or thing is a pattern of meaning, an abbreviated description, definition or set of 'facts' concerning the thing in question; typically prescribing an event, object, feeling, etc.; in token of, as a sign, symbol, or evidence of something.

DEFENCE-IN-DEPTH—an approach to comprehensive information security—whereby network privacy is protected by means of nested protective layers—and the same—which may include stealth defences for closing/blocking/camouflaging access-gateways, plus multiple layers of encryption/coding and layered symbolic, meaning and selectional gateways etc.

Descriptive Content—refers to matching each symbol in a representation to its specific meaning—and according to the common descriptive language employed.

Descriptive Attack-Surface—Relates to Descriptive Content— whereby notably the sender and receiver may be using an obscure coding language whereby the symbol-to-meaning relationship is protected (i.e. red means big etc).

Datum-Copy—is a particular instantiation of a datum's pattern— that exists inside or (potentially) outside of a point-to-point communication system. Creation of a datum-copy involves instantiation of form in place and time (i.e. illustration of content in the real and/or virtual worlds). A datum-copy is a particular instantiation of a datum's pattern—that exists inside or (potentially) outside of a point-to-point communication system.

Datum Meaning—refers to the de-coded meaning content present in a datum's content; or to the specific ideas/concepts that are to be conveyed.

DIGI-GRAPH (Greek: di, 'twice' + graphic, 'to write')—An encipherment in which the plain-text is written using letter pairs.

DISTRIBUTED TRANSPORT—refers to the process of distributed transport for digital packets—whereby in terms of a single point-to-point communication instance—data-packets are routed along different network paths—and hence through different servers (normally reflection servers).

ENCRYPTION (Symbolic)—Symbolic Encryption is the process of encrypting symbolic messages—or obfuscating datums consisting of patterns of symbols. Whereby information is encoded in such a way that only authorised parties can read it—typically by replacing/jumbling symbols according to a mathematical procedure which obscures the original symbolic pattern. In an encryption scheme, the intended communication of information, referred to as plaintext (i.e "Alan is tall"), is encrypted using a special algorithm, generating cipher-text that can only be read if decrypted (i.e."Bmbo jl umm").

ENTITY AUTHENTICATION / IDENTIFICATION— Corroboration of the identity of an entity (e.g a person, a computer terminal etc).

ENVIRONMENTAL SPYING—spying on the primary-network through leaking emanations, including radio or electrical signals and vibration(s) etc.

EXPLOIT (SECURITY SYSTEM)—An exploit is a piece of software, a chunk of data, or a sequence of commands that takes advantage of a bug or vulnerability (via an Access Gateway) in order to cause unintended or unanticipated behaviour to occur on a computer system's software, hardware, or something electronic.

Form (Datum-Copy)—A copy has two primary aspects: firstly form (the encapsulating media of storage / communication / delivery / access) and secondly—content (see definition).

FRONT-DOOR—is an open access-gateway that may be accessed by legitimate users; or else 'hacked'/broken-into by illegitimate users; ergo a front-door enables actors to bypass network security system(s) and obtain access to private datum(s).

GEOMETRIC PATTERNS—Configurations used to align, transpose or substitute alphabet letters with other letters, numerals or special forms such as those of symbol cryptography.

HACKING—In the computer security context, a hacker is someone who seeks and exploits weaknesses in a computer system or network. Hackers may be motivated by a multitude of reasons, such as profit, protest, challenge, enjoyment, or to evaluate those weaknesses to assist in removing them.

IDENTITY MANAGEMENT—describes the management of individual identities (matching unique and specific human(s))—and their authentication and authorisation—plus privileges within or across system and enterprise boundaries with the goal of increasing security and productivity while decreasing cost, downtime and repetitive tasks.

Illegitimate Secondary Copy—is a secondary-copy that is/has-been created by an unwarranted party (or actor)—effectively a system hacker—the same being one who does not have permission to do the same, and/or to access the contained private datum(s).

INTERNET-PROTOCOL (IP)—is the principal communications protocol in the Internet protocol suite for relaying datagrams across network boundaries. Each access device on the Internet is assigned a semi-unique (but possibly temporary) IP address for the purposes of identification during local and remote communication(s).

Invitation-Only Network—A special type of network design in which members are required to invite each other onto respective private networks—whereby whilst the system may exist on an open network—communications on the invitation network cannot be made with non-members.

JARGON CODES—Open methods of linguistic concealment. A type of open code, the jargon code is not hidden by symbols or transposed letters. Rather, an innocent word or words replaces another term in a sentence constructed in an innocuous fashion.

KeyMail—Multi-encrypted P2P electronic mail protocol (developed by Alan Radley) that provides Absolute Security (ref. target and methods).

Legitimate Secondary Copy—is a secondary-copy that is/has-been created by a warranted party (or actor)—often the network system itself (e.g central-server copies) the same being one who has permission to do the same.

Local-Actor—A local-actor is a data processing unit—existing on a local access-device—comprised of either hardware and/or software elements—which (potentially) acts on a datum-copy's form and/or content within the primary-network's data-processing stack.

MAC ADDRESS—A unique identifier for a computer and/or other networked device (typically for use on an open-network such as the Internet).

MALWARE—is an umbrella term used to refer to a variety of forms of hostile or intrusive software, including computer viruses, worms, trojan horses, ransomware, spyware, adware, scareware, and other malicious programs. It can take the form of executable code, scripts, active content, and other software.

Meaning Gateway—an access-gateway that protects who (i.e. which human and/or automatic actor) can decode the meaning of a datum-copy's inner representation/information. May consist of metrical (symbolic), descriptive, and selectional layers.

Memory Node—A computer node that acts as a storage medium for a Datum-Copy.

MESSAGE AUTHENTICATION—Corroborating the source of the information; also know as data origin authentication.

MESSAGE—The information pattern/datum-content to be transferred.

Metrical Content—For any representation, notably, the metrical aspect—or pattern of atomic facts/symbols—is always present—and works together with a descriptive aspect—to convey meaning.

Metrical Attack-Surface—Consists of a pattern of atomic facts/symbols used to convey meaning.

NSA—National Security Agency (USA).

Network-Actor—A network-actor is a data processing unit—existing on a remote networked-device—comprised of either hardware and/or software elements—which (potentially) acts on a datum-copy's form and/or content within the primary-network's data-processing stack.

NULL—A meaningless letter, symbol or number inserted into a code list or cypher alphabet. Nulls are used to complicate decryption efforts of unintended 3rd-parties; by disrupting sentence patterns, word lengths and the frequency of syllable groups.

ONE-TIME-PAD—In cryptography the one-time pad (OTP) is an encryption technique that cannot be cracked if used correctly. In this technique, a plaintext is paired with a random secret key (also referred to as a one-time pad). Then, each bit or character of the plaintext is encrypted by combining it with the corresponding bit or character from the pad using modular addition. If the key is truly random, is at least as long as the plaintext, is never reused in whole or in part, and is kept completely secret, then the resulting cipher-text will be impossible to decrypt or break. However, practical problems have (often) prevented one-time pads from being widely used. The "pad" part of the name comes from early implementations where the key material was distributed as a pad of paper, so that the top sheet could be easily torn off and destroyed after use.

OPEN CODE—A code concealed in an apparently innocent message. Open codes are a branch of linguistically masked communications which includes null cyphers, geometric methods and jargon codes.

Open-Datum—is one that anyone may access—but open-thoughts are not a subject of this book (see Self-as-Computer).

Open-Network—refers to a network (such as the Internet) in which any number of access-nodes/devices may be connected and/or inter-communicate with few top-level rules—but only lower-level protocols. Traffic flows across an open network without any restrictions/controls.

PATTERN OBFUSCATION—refers to special encryption/coding/scrambling methods—employed to prevent spies from deducing information from patterns present in the copy.

PEER-TO-PEER or P2P NETWORK—such as Napster, BitCoin, BitTorrent etc; the same forming a distributed network of peer-to-peer nodes that render the communicated information directly available to network participants—without the need for centralised co-ordination. A key advantage of P2P is that 'participating users establish a virtual network, entirely independent from the physical network, without having to obey any administrative authorities or restrictions.'

Partial Security—defined as a network which may possibly produce—or cause to come into existence—any unprotected—or nth-party accessible—primary/secondary/tertiary datum-copies.

PERFECT SECURITY—is the notion that, given an encrypted message (or cipher-text) from a perfectly secure encryption system (or cipher), absolutely nothing will be revealed about the unencrypted message (or plaintext) by the cipher-text.

PERFECT FORWARD SECURITY—is a feature of specific key agreement protocols that gives assurances your session keys will not be compromised even if the private key of the server is compromised.

Physical Gateway—refers to access-gateways related to the copy's physical representation—for example any gateways existing on media of storage, access and/or transport.

Physical Representation (Datum-Copy)—refers to an electronic/magnetic/optical 'container' for a datum-copy.

Primary-Copy—is a place-holder for a private datum of meaning—existing within the boundaries of a point-to-point communication system; whose content and form are restricted in terms of social access (i.e who can see, know & change the same); whereby the datum is (ideally) communicated via single-copy-send from the source point to any (and all) designated receiver point(s).

Primary-Network—is a provided point-to-point communication system; whereby a private access-node (the source point) exists on a networked access-device; which stores a primary-copy of a private-datum; prior to the single-copy-send of the same to a socially restricted access-node (the destination-point). A primary-network may create legitimate secondary-copies of the primary-copy.

PRIVACY—is defined as social restriction of an item (ie. an idea/thought/datum-copy etc) to two or more parties alone—whereby access to any related copies are protected/restricted for any and all other unwarranted persons/actors.

Private Communication—can be defined as protection of privacy of meaning; or the safe transfer of single/multiple datum(s) between humans.

Private-Datum — A private-thought/datum is distributed/available to a limited number of people; and hence some form of social sharing plus protection is implied; and in order to prevent it from morphing into an open-thought/datum.

Private-Thoughts — Thoughts which are shared amongst a restricted group of people.

Private-by-Guarantee — Maintenance of privacy for an item for an extended period of time — whereby there is no possibility of the item morphing into an open one — in terms of social access.

PUBLIC KEY ENCRYPTION — the (public) encryption key is published for anyone to use and encrypt messages. However, only the receiving party has access to the (private) decryption key that allows messages to be read.

Reflection (packet routing) Server — A server (existing on a communication network) which merely 'reflect's or directs packets from one location to another — and does not store any of these packets on the same server for extended periods of time.

SCRAMBLING (Data) — Jumbling and/or changing the order of a datum(s) symbols according to an (ostensibly) unreadable scheme and/or algorithm.

SCRAMBLING (Channel) — Jumbling and/or changing the order of a communication's data packets according to an (ostensibly) unreadable scheme and/or algorithm.

Secondary-Copy — is a replication of a primary-copy — existing within (or outside) the boundaries of a point-to-point communication system — that may be legitimately produced by the communication process itself; and/or be illegitimately created as a result of the unwarranted activities of a hacker.

Secondary-Network — is a privileged-access network intimately connected to the primary-network's communication pipeline; whereby copies of communicated private-datum(s) may exist on an nth-party organisational network and/or various local and/or central replication (backup) network(s). A secondary-network may contain legitimate replicated secondary-copies of primary-copies and/or other secondary-copies.

SECRET-KEY—In cryptography, a private or secret key is an encryption/decryption key known only to the party or parties that exchange secret messages. In traditional secret key cryptography, a key would be shared by the communicators so that each could encrypt and decrypt messages.

SECRET-KEY MANAGEMENT—Protective methods for a specific secret-key—in order to protect the key from unwarranted social access.

Secret-Datum—(analogous to a secret-thought)—which has not yet left the source point (or sender's mind); and which is assumed to be unique in that nobody else can know (or discover) the precise form or content of the datum at the source point.

SECURITY—Accordingly, security—for a person-to-person communication system—can be defined as protection of secrecy, privacy or openness of meaning; or the safe transfer of single/multiple datum(s) between humans.

SECURITY BUG—A **security bug** or security defect is a software bug that can be exploited to gain unauthorized access or privileges on a computer system. Security bugs introduce security vulnerabilities by compromising one or more of:

- Authentication of users and other entities
- Authorisation of access-rights and privileges
- Data Confidentiality (Privacy, Secrecy)
- Data Integrity

Security bugs need not be identified nor exploited to qualify as such.

Selectional Content—refers to modal context(s) with respect to a representation—or modal constructive aspect(s) of the same.

Selectional Attack Surface—refers to a protective layer for any selectional (modal) context(s) present—and hence to the (potential) opening-up of any constructive aspect(s) for the representation.

Self-Computer—Merging of human(s) with computers, machines, systems and technology.

SEMAGRAM—A form of steganography, wherein encryptions are made of arrangements of objects, images, or symbols rather than by letters or numbers.

SHANNON'S MAXIM—(i.e. Kerckhoff's principle); assume that: 'the enemy knows the system'.Avoid relying on security through obscurity and/or security through minority—in terms of assuming that the secrecy/uncommonness of system design provides unimpeachable protection.

SIGNATURE—A means to bind information to an entity.

Social Access—refers to humans gaining access to a datum-copy's form and or content.

Stealth Network—refers to any network that employs stealth techniques and/or defensive mechanisms—to protect-against/repeal—any unwarranted hackers/attacks; and in terms of excluding/disguising/blocking entry-point(s) for the primary-network's data-processing stack.

Single-Copy-Send—communication of a datum (+ meta-data) with guaranteed social security.

Socially Secure Communication—communication that protects socially restricted access (secrecy or privacy) for the replicated meaning—datum(s) + nominal meta-data (perhaps).

SPYING—refers to secret/unwarranted access to private items/ideas/datum(s)/concepts etc.

STEGANOGRAPHY—(Greek: steganos, 'covered' + graphein, 'writing')—A primary form of communications security that conceals the physical presence of a secret message, which may or may not be additionally protected by a code or cipher.

Storage Media—is a bundle of hardware/software technologies that work together to form a memory system—and in order to persist a datum-copy's form and content.

SYMMETRIC KEY ENCRYPTION—the encryption and decryption keys are the same. Communicating parties must have the same key before they can achieve secure communication.

Tertiary-Copy—is a replication of a primary or secondary copy—which is generated post-communication by extracting datum(s) from a large body of communication data (e.g. a transatlantic data pipe).

Tertiary-Network—is not directly connected to the primary-network—but nevertheless may still (belatedly) access data traffic flowing across primary and/or secondary-networks—resulting in illegitimate tertiary-copies of primary/secondary-copies.

Transfer Media—is a bundle of hardware/software technologies that work together to form a delivery system—and in order to send a datum-copy from a source-point to a destination-point.

TRANSMISSIONS SECURITY—An electronic form of communication security similar to steganography. Transmission security tries to hide the existence of secret messages in electrical exchanges, whether or not they are encrypted.

TROJAN HORSE—unsafe-actors misrepresenting as safe-actors.

UNBREAKABLE CIPHERS—include one-time methods and unconditionally secure crypto-systems.

Unsafe-Actor—An actor on the data-processing stack that is invisible/unknown/questionable in terms of purpose and/or integrity—and hence may (potentially) have undermined effects and/or progress unknown programming path(s).

USER-IDENTITY (ID)—individual identity for an actor on a network (perhaps matching unique/specific human(s)).

VALIDATION—A means to provide timeliness of authorisation to use or manipulate information or resources.

Virtual Representation (Datum-Copy)—refers to what is stored on an electronic/magnetic/optical 'container' for a datum-copy (information).

Virtual Gateway—refers to blocking mechanisms/hurdles with respect to the opening-up of a virtual representation of a datum-copy.

VIRUS (computer)—is a malware program that, when executed, replicates by inserting copies of itself (possibly modified) into other programs, data files etc , and when this replication succeeds, the affected areas are then said to be 'infected'. A virus may or may not have harmful effects—and result in loss of privacy for private datum(s) etc.

VULNERABILITY—In **computer** security, a **vulnerability** is a weakness which allows an attacker to reduce a system's information assurance. **Vulnerability** is the intersection of three elements: a system susceptibility or flaw, attacker access to the flaw, and attacker capability to exploit the flaw.

Cybersecurity Axioms

[Axiom 1] Datum: A datum of any idea or thing is a pattern of meaning, an abbreviated description, definition or set of 'facts' concerning the thing in question; typically prescribing an event, object, feeling, etc.; in token of, as a sign, symbol, or evidence of something.

[Axiom 2] Datum Expression/Source: Datums are typically expressed within the boundaries of a specific language, medium, media and/or code; and normally each datum has an inherent lifetime whereby it may be created, stored, communicated, replicated, lost and/or destroyed etc. Each datum has a human and/or machine creator/author, plus normally human owner(s) and user(s) (ref. social accessibility (or privacy) status).

[Axiom 3] Datum Types: Datums come in three kinds:

- A private datum is accessible only by a restricted group of people—or a particular set of human beings; and is inaccessible to all other persons [Axiom 3.1].
- A secret datum is accessible only by a single human being—typically the owner and often the author; and is inaccessible to all other persons [Axiom 3.2].
- An open datum is (potentially) accessible by anyone— or by an unrestricted group of people [Axiom 3.3].

[Axiom 4] Communication System: A communication system is a system or facility for transferring datum(s)/patterns-of-meaning between persons and equipment. The system usually consists of a collection of individual communication networks, transmission systems, relay stations, tributary stations and terminal equipment capable of interconnection and interoperation so as to form an integrated whole.

[Axiom 5] SECURITY: Security for a person-to-person communication system—can be defined as protection of secrecy, privacy or openness of meaning; or the safe transfer of single/multiple datum(s) between human(s).

[Axiom 6] Social Accessibility (Privacy) Status: The ability of a person to see, know and/or change a datum's form and/or content.

[Axiom 7] Protect = Lock, Block or Conceal an item.

[Axiom 8] Single-Copy-Send: Henceforth adjudging that a point-to-point communication is private and secure; is equivalent to saying that the original unit of meaning existing at the 'source' node has, as a result of the one-to-one replication, only one accessible copy—at the 'receiver' node. Furthermore this copy is—unequivocally—accessible only by the (trusted) human for whom the communication was intended (i.e. it is access-controlled).We call such a process single-copy-send— or socially secure communication.

[Axiom 8.1] Meta-Data: Whereby the process of communication may itself be private (no public meta-data exists); and there is no possibility of any nth-party obtaining a copy of the communicated datum.

[Axiom 9] Primary-Copy: A primary-copy is a place-holder for a private datum of meaning—existing within the boundaries of a point-to-point communication system; whose content and form are restricted in terms of social access (i.e who can see, know & change the same); whereby the datum is (ideally) communicated via single-copy-send from the source-point to any (and all) designated receiver-point(s).

[Axiom 10] Secondary-Copy: A secondary-copy is a (communicated/backup) replication of a primary-copy—existing within (or outside) the boundaries of a point-to-point communication system—that may be legitimately produced by the communication process itself (e.g. a central server copy); and/or be illegitimately created as a result of the unwarranted activities of a hacker.

[Axiom 11] Tertiary-Copy: A tertiary-copy is a replication of a primary or secondary copy—which is generated post-communication by extracting datum(s) from a large body of communication data (e.g. a transatlantic data pipe).

[Axiom 12] Absolute Security Target: For a point-to-point communication instance—is the replication of a single instance (or primary-copy) of a private-datum from one socially restricted access-node to another [ref. Absolute Security:TARGET]. In other words, it is the single-copy-send of a datum from one party to another; whereby no—socially accessible—nth-party copies exist whatsoever (hopefully persistently—or on a long-term basis).

[Axiom 13] Partial/Absent Security: Likewise we can define partial/absent security as the existence of any unprotected—or nth-party accessible—primary/secondary/tertiary datum-copies.

[Axiom 14] Digital Media: Digital-media are electronic media used to store, transmit and receive digitised information; and may refer to any media that has been encoded in a machine-readable format. Digital-media—or simply media—can be created, viewed, distributed, modified and preserved on computers. For our purposes we have compartmentalised media into three types: storage, transfer and access.

[Axiom 15] Datum-Copy: A datum is a discrete pattern of meaning that may be transferred between minds (network access-nodes). A datum-copy is a particular instantiation of a datum's pattern—that exists inside or (potentially) outside of a point-to-point communication system. A copy has two primary aspects: firstly form (the encapsulating format)—or media of storage, communication/delivery, and access; and secondly content (a representation with metrical, descriptive and selectional aspects).

[Axiom 16] Datum-Copy Ownership: A datum-copy has a natural owner—often the sender/creator of the datum.

[Axiom 17] Ownership Rights: Ownership rights include protection of social access (e.g. secrecy, privacy, openness) for the copy—in terms of who can see, know and/or change the content and/or form of the copy (ref. new owner(s)/user(s)).

[Axiom 18] Hacking: When we speak of—a datum-copy being hacked and/or a data-breach/system-exploit occurring—that is defined as unwarranted social access to the informational content of the datum (i.e. loss/change of privacy status.

[Axiom 19] Coherent Defence: Previously, for an act of private communication, we had assumed that a local access-node provided socially restricted access to primary-copies. However such a statement is predicated on the fact that each access-device affords an actor-coherent defence against any data-breaches—successfully.

[Axiom 20] Network Term And Hybrid Actors: Use of the term 'network'—is problematic to say the least. This is because an access-device may be open to the data-processing activities of (any number of) inter-relating local-actors plus network-actors (i.e. human/automated ones etc). Ergo hybrid-actors are formed that may be partially/fully invisible, overly complex, and/or unknowable in some way—and which may be—as yet—only potentially present.

[Axiom 21] Datum's Context Of Use: A datum's content may have a purely informational meaning (be descriptive) and/or a purely logical meaning (be functional)—or posses a combination of both kinds of meaning—according to context of use. However, the process of point-to-point transfer of a datum; is (normally) defined to be a transfer of information alone—and the datum (content) is immutable.

[Axiom 22] Datum Replication: Replication of a primary-copy (datum from + content) is transfer to a destination-point. It may be that a copy's form (encapsulating media of storage, communication/delivery, and access etc) changes during replication—hence (datum) copies are mutable (form aspects).

[Axiom 23] Protection Methods: There are basically three ways to defend/protect an item in the real-world. For example, when protecting an entrance to a house (i.e. walled safe)—we can:

1   Lock the entrance and armour reinforce it—or make it difficult to open/know;
2   Block the entrance pathway—by preventing an attacker from reaching it—for example by placing objects in the entrance-way—or by eliminating it altogether;
3   Conceal the entrance—and make it difficult to see/find.

Similarly for datum-copies/attack-surfaces—we can protect these in analogous way(s)

[Axiom 24] Coherency Predicates: We can identify two—enforced—coherency predicates for Absolute Security; namely: actor-unity (of purpose); and actor-integrity (of action); for safe hardware/software operations on each access-device.

[Axiom 25] Data-Processing Legitimacy: Similarly, unsafe-actor repellent/containment techniques can be used to preserve the legitimacy of data-processing operation(s) on the primary-network.

[Axiom 26] Attack-Surface Types: Attack-surfaces come in six basic kinds.

Firstly we have three related to the datum-copy's form; or its encapsulating media of storage, transfer and access. Secondly we have three attack-surface types related to the datum-copy's content; and these are the metrical, descriptive and selectional ones.

[Axiom 27] Actor: An actor (i.e. a program/human/process) existing on and/or influencing the data-processing stack that may be structurally—visible/invisible and/or known/unknown in terms of existence—but remain questionable/harmful in terms of purpose, value, action and/or integrity—and hence may (potentially) cause undetermined/detrimental/harmful effects and/or progress unknown or undesirable programming path(s); or else provide unauthorised access to private-datum(s) etc.

[Axiom 28] Datum-Copy Components: A datum-copy—encapsulated on a media device—has three components: two related to form: the physical representation, and the virtual representation, and one related to content: which is the meaning representation (with the aforementioned metrical, descriptive and selectional aspects).

[Axiom 29] Protective Measures/Types: Ergo, there are 5 possible attack-surface types for each of three possible media of storage, transfer and access—leading to a grand total of 15 attack-surface types. However each surface may be protected by 6 kinds of protection (entry-method(s) + defence-method(s)): or locking, blocking and concealment mechanism(s); hence we can have up to 90 fundamental kinds/types of protection for a single copy (or a private datum).

[Axiom 30] Local Actor: A local-actor is a data processing unit—existing on a local access-device—comprised of either hardware and/or software/human elements—which (potentially) acts on a datum-copy's form and/or content within the primary-network's data-processing stack.

[Axiom 31] Network-Actor: A network-actor is a data processing unit—existing on a remote networked-device—comprised of either hardware and/or software/human elements—which (potentially) acts on a datum-copy's form and/or content within the primary-network's data-processing stack.

[Axiom 32] Actor-Coherent Defence: An actor-coherent defence is when all of the actors, entities and processes—present in a primary-network's data-processing stack—are impelled to act together in order to protect the private datum-copy's form and/or content from unwarranted social access (hopefully for all places/times). N.B. An actor may originate—from either automated processes and/or human ones.

[Axiom 33] Access-Node: An access-node is a virtual access gateway (i.e. legitimate login-node/point-of-entry) for a primary/secondary/tertiary network; and is normally used (only) by an authorised party to gain entry to said network. An access-device is a physical access device that enables a human to gain entry to the same network (i.e. a personal computer).

[Axiom 34] Primary-Network: The primary-network is a provided point-to-point communication system; whereby a private access-node (the source-point) exists on a networked access-device; which stores a primary-copy of a private-datum; prior to the single-copy-send of the same to a socially restricted access-node (the destination-point). A primary-network may create legitimate secondary-copies of the primary-copy.

[Axiom 35] Secondary-Network: A secondary-network is a privileged-access network intimately connected to the primary-network's communication pipeline; whereby copies of communicated private-datum(s) may exist on an nth-party organisational network and/or various local and/or central replication (backup) network(s). A secondary-network may contain legitimate replicated secondary-copies of primary-copies and/or other secondary-copies.

[Axiom 36] Tertiary-Network: A tertiary-network is not directly connected to the primary-network—but nevertheless may still (belatedly) access data traffic flowing across primary and/or secondary-networks—resulting in illegitimate tertiary-copies of primary/secondary-copies.

[Axiom 37] Metrical Attack-Surface: The so-called metrical attack-surface may be protected (for example) by means of encryption (entry locks + content concealment)—or obfuscation of symbolic structure—and so that only an actor with the correct unlocking algorithm(s)/key(s) can decode the underlying symbolic pattern.

[Axiom 38] Descriptive Attack-Surface: The metrical layer is decoded, we must match each symbol to its specific meaning—and according to the common descriptive language employed—named the descriptive attack-surface.

[Axiom 39] Selectional Attack-Surface: Notably the sender and receiver may be using an obscure coding language whereby the symbol-to-meaning relationship is protected (i.e. RED means BIG etc). Finally, modal context(s)—named selectional attack-surface(s)—may protect constructive aspect(s) of the representation.

[Axiom 40] Concealment: We have the target (item to be concealed); and the concealment method. Whereby there are two basic kinds of concealment structural targets: existence of the item, and content (or inner meaning).

[Axiom 41] Concealment Structure: Structure can be—CONCEALED—in 3 ways·

1   Conceal form itself; or
2   Conceal location (where); or
3   Conceal location (when): item time-span, duration or persistence.

[Axiom 42] Concealment Methods: Whereby there are 3 basic processes: (for each method/way)

1   Conceal by transformation of form/location; or
2   Conceal by similarity (equivalency)—that is by hiding an item alongside a large number (of ostensibly identical) items; and
3   Conceal by difference (complexity)—or hiding an item amongst a large number of greatly/potentially varying forms/structures.

[Axiom 43] Attack-Surface/Window: An attack-surface /attack-window is an exposed facet/system entry-point for a datum-copy, existing on a primary-network's data-processing stack, and which (potentially) facilitates unwarranted social access to a private datum-copy's content and/or form.

[Axiom 44] Attack-Vector: An attack-vector is a specific data-processing path, existing on a primary-network's data-processing stack—which (potentially) provides unwarranted social access to a private datum-copy's content and/or form.

[Axiom 45] Access-Gateway: An access-gateway consists of one or more access-nodes and/or exposed attack-surface(s)/window(s)—for a primary, secondary or tertiary copy.

[Axiom 46] Storage-Media: A storage-media is a bundle of hardware/software technologies that work together to form a memory system—and in order to persist a datum-copy's form and content.

[Axiom 47] Transfer-Media: A transfer-media is a bundle of hardware/software technologies that work together to form a delivery system—and in order to send a datum-copy from a source-point to a destination-point.

[Axiom 48] Access-Media: An access-media is a hardware/software system that enables an actor to see, know and/or change a copy's form and/or content (e.g. a data-access terminal).

[Axiom 49] Concealment Target: There are basically two kinds of concealment targets; you can either focus on concealing structure—or else encourage the observer to look elsewhere (still a form of concealment).

Whereby either the onlooker:

1   Does not know where or when to look for an item (target location obfuscation); or secondly:
2   Finds that looking does not reveal how to find the item (target form confusion); or finally:
3   Is encouraged to look elsewhere than an item's true location (observer-misdirection—i.e. concentrate on directing the attention of the observer—using decoys and/or false targets—or hide messages in innocuous content etc).

[Axiom 50] For Absolute Security, we must protect:

1   Physical-Gateway(s)—who can obtain a physical copy.
2   Virtual-Gateway(s)—who can open a virtual copy.
3   Meaning-Gateway(s)—who can decode datum(s).

To be successful, an intruder must first pass through the physical and virtual gateway(s); prior to deciphering the meaning of the inner datum(s)—or passing through any meaning-gateway(s) that happen to be present.

[Axiom 51] Locking Mechanisms: Just for clarification— herein whenever we speak of a locking mechanism for a datum-copy (existing on a specific media of storage, transfer and access)—what we are saying is that the lock prevents the knowing/opening action (i.e for datum access)—by some protected entry-method plus defence-method(s) (i.e. password entry-system (lock) plus content concealment of symbolic structure) [Axiom 51.1].

Alternatively, existence concealment prevents an unsafe-actor from seeing/finding a copy by means of an entry-method that is itself secret/hidden (i.e. unusual descriptive coding) and/or secret/hidden defence-method(s) (e.g. possibly identical to entry-method) [Axiom 51.2]. Likewise for blocking actions (ref. reaching) [Axiom 51.2]. Obviously there is overlap (and nesting) between the concepts of lock, block and conceal—but it is often useful to open-up protection—as a concept—into such facets.

[**Axiom 52**] **Cryptographic Principles:** Ergo, we abide by one (or more) of the following-

CRYPTOGRAPHIC PRINCIPLES:

- Principle A – Virtual Message Tamper-proofing: The digital signature verification and encryption must be applied to the cipher-text—when it is created—typically on the same primary-network used to compose the message—to avoid tampering (adequate locking—guarantees message integrity).
- Principle B – Physical Message Tamper-proofing: Encrypting at the time of creation is only secure if the encryption device itself has not been tampered with (i.e. closed/blocked physical gateway(s) or device-integrity).
- Principle C – Employ Secret Keys: Obey Dr Claude Shannon's maxim (i.e. Kerckhoff's principle); and assume that: 'the enemy knows the system'. Avoid relying on security through obscurity and/or security through minority—in terms of not assuming that the secrecy/uncommonness of system design provides unimpeachable protection (adequate concealment + locking).
- Principle D – Pattern Obfuscation: Special encryption/coding/scrambling methods must be employed to prevent spies from deducing information from patterns present in the copy.

- Principle E – Access-node/Key/ID Security: Adequate access control methods must be employed to protect unwarranted access to any and all access-nodes, access-devices, keys, user IDs etc (adequate blocking + key concealment).

- Principle F – Viruses, Trojan-Horses: Methods to eradicate Viruses and to prohibit Trojans misrepresenting as safe-actors—hence preventing unsafe-actors from gaining unwarranted access to copies/actors on the data-processing stack (adequate blocking).

- Principle G – Environmental Spying: Methods to prevent spying on the primary-network through leaking emanations, including radio or electrical signals and vibration(s) etc.

[Axiom 53] Protection By Diversity: Protection by Diversity is a fundamental principle for attaining secrecy/privacy; whereby we first block/bar entry to a private item by some defensive means or protective barrier. Next we build a window/door into the barrier that may be opened (i.e. know/open action)—but only by means of a fully/partially secret entry-method. The entry-method typically includes a mathematical/text value and/or locking key (i.e. a secret password) with a specific form known/available only to authorised parties—and that is difficult to attain/guess; whereby it is diversity (potential to have many different values) that protects the key from discovery/use by an attacker.

[Axiom 54] Coding Types: Descriptive coding refers to the process of assigning a pattern of symbols to the specific meaning of the conveyed message (communicated datum(s)). Selective coding refers to the process of protecting constructive aspects of the symbolic and/or descriptive components of the message by means of private modal context(s).

[Axiom 55] Coding Principles: Ergo—for socially secure communication—we abide by—as many as possible of—the following message/datum CODING PRINCIPLES:

CODING PRINCIPLES

1   Employ effective symbolic encryption; including multi-layer encryption with new keys generated for each communication instance (i.e. use perfect-forward-secrecy).
2   Employ obscure descriptive coding methods (i.e. one-time-pad(s) or perfect-secrecy).
3   Employ variable selectional coding methods (i.e. multiple code-books in a single message); with constantly changing constructive pattern(s) for each message. (i.e. one-time-pad(s) or perfect-secrecy).
4   Employ safe pattern constructs. Avoid sending identical (coded) natural-language constructs repetitively; pad the pattern(s) with NULLS or hide them; use varying constructive code(s).
5   Rely on the Beholder's Share—employ covert and obscure methods for interpretation of meaning.

[Axiom 56] Evasion Attacks: In network security, evasion is bypassing network security in order to deliver an exploit, attack, or other form of malware to a target network or system, without detection.

[Axiom 57] Stealth Defences: A nice antipodal proposition—and remedy for—an evasive attack—is a stealth defence. Whereby all physical and virtual system gateways are rendered invisible and/or out-of-reach of the data-processing actions of any harmful attackers.

[Axiom 58] Gateway Protection: A good rule-of-thumb for achieving—socially secure communication—is that it is always easier (and more effective) to eliminate/conceal a system gateway than to protect access to the same gateway.

[Axiom 59] Stealth Techniques: Effective—STEALTH TECHNIQUES—include (for defence):

STEALTH TECHNIQUES

- BLOCK – Move access-node(s)—plus related data-set(s)—including user data (i.e. user owned IDs/keys)—to a private (possibly portable) access-device; closing physical/virtual gateway(s).
- RESTRICT– Employ an invitation-only-network + cypher-matching—whereby unsafe parties are blocked (i.e use a private network).
- DECEPTION – Use false/null data-traffic, decoys, honey-pots, spoofed access-device IP/MAC addresses (hide source + destination IDs/point(s)); hide message(s) in innocuous content; closing invalid gateway(s).
- SECRECY – Use a secret/scrambled/coded protocol (key-protected); secret routers/gateways—to close/protect all datum physical/virtual-gateway(s).
- CURTAIL – Eliminate all legitimate and illegitimate secondary copies (e.g. use a Peer-to-Peer (P2P) network); closing physical + virtual gateway(s).
- DEFEND – Protect the communication channel (e.g. use distributed transport and/or concealed packet(s)).
- CONCEAL – Conceal the method(s) of coding within a large range of possible method(s) + vary/overlap method(s); that is protect meaning gateway(s) (i.e. exploit the beholder's share).
- LOCALISE – Localise Identity and Access Management System(s). Do not trust private items to nth-parties.
- CONFUSE – Employ nested protective layers (ref. physical/virtual gateways).

[Axiom 60] Gateway Protection: In a nutshell, we wish to reduce gateway: exposure (limit existence in place/time), number(s), visibility and fragility—eliminating/nullifying attack-vectors.

[Axiom 61] Gateway Architecture: As previously defined, an access-gateway consists of one or more access-nodes and/or (potentially) exposed attack-surfaces for a primary, secondary or tertiary copy. Earlier in Chapter 6 we characterised three different types of access-gateway for datum-copies existing on a point-to-point communication system. Firstly, we have physical-gateway(s)—which determine who may obtain a physical copy; next we have virtual-gateway(s)—which determine who can open a virtual/formatted copy; and finally we have meaning-gateway(s) that determine who can decode a copy. To be successful an intruder must (typically) pass through several (nested) physical and virtual gateway(s); before decoding all meaning gateway(s)—and in order to uncover the communicated datum(s). Ergo gateway defence-method(s) and/or entry-barriers—typically provide a hierarchy of defensive 'high-walls'—much like a castle (defence-in-depth).

[Axiom 62] Absolute Security (Target and Methods): In summary, attaining Absolute Security for our digital communication(s)—is a difficult-to-reach—but not impossible goal. Just like the magician, rather than performing any real magic tricks (achieving unbreakable encryption/coding)—we misdirect.

Accordingly, we seek to:

1   Lock/block/conceal system gateway(s);
2   Conceal the method(s) of entry/defence (variable aspects) within a large range—of(potential) methods;
3   Employ depth-defences to confuse/slow-down an attacker.

In this manner (A+B+C) [named as Axiom 62], we safeguard attack-surface entry-methods.

END OF LISTING OF SCF VERSION 1.0 – CYBERSECURITY AXIOMS

****

Notes

INTRODUCTION

1. Lanwehr, Carl.: Cybersecurity: From Engineering to Science, *NSA Review of Emerging Technologies, The Next Wave, Volume 19. no 2.* (2012).
2. Lanwehr, Carl.: *What would a scientific foundation for a cybersecurity science look like?, NSA Review of Emerging Technologies, Volume 19, no2.* (2012).

COMMUNICATIONS SECURITY

1. Levy, S.: *How the NSA nearly destroyed the Internet.* Wired. (January 2014)
2. Veltman, K.: *The Alphabets of Life.* (2014)
3. Lanier, J.: *Who Owns the Future.* (2013)
4. Bush, V.: *As We May Think. The Atlantic.* (1945)
5. Otlet, P.: Monde: *Essai d'universalisme.* (1935)
6. Veltman, K.: *Understanding New Media.* (2006)
7. Gibson, W.: *Neuromancer.* (1984)
8. Berners-Lee, T.: *Weaving the Web.* (1999)
9. Berners-Lee, T.: *World wide Web needs bill of rights.* On-line BBC News article. (12 March 2014)(http://www.bbc.co.uk/news/uk-26540635) Accesses 9 April 2014.
10. Rheingold, H.: *Tools for Thought.* MIT Press. (1983)
11. Rucker, R.: *Mind Tools.* Penguin Books. (1987)
12. Landauer, T.K.: *The Trouble with Computers . MIT Press.* (1996)
13. Licklider, J.C.R.: *Man-Computer Symbiosis.* (1960)
14. Engelbart, E.: *Augmenting Human Intellect: A Conceptual Framework.* (1962)
15. Kurzweil, R.: *The Singularity is Near.* (2005)
16. Carroll, J.B.: *Language, Thought and Reality.* (1956)
17. Radley, A.: Computers as Self., Proceedings of the 4th International Conference in Human-Computer Interaction, Tourism and Cultural Heritage, (2013).
18. Radley, A.: Self as Computer—2015.
19. Radley, A.: Humans versus Computers Systems and Machines; a Battle for Freedom, Equality and Democracy, keynote paper, Proceedings of the 6th International Conference in Human-Computer Interaction, Tourism and Cultural Heritage, (2015).
20. Shannon, Claude, E.: *A Mathematical Theory of Communication.* (1949)
21. Shannon, Claude, E.: Theory of Secret Systems.
22. Rivest, Ronald, A Method for Obtaining Digital Signatures and Public Key Encryption CryptoSystems.
23. MacKay, Donald, Information, Mechanism and Meaning, The MIT Press, 1969

WHY SECURITY IS ALL ABOUT COPIES

1. Wrixen, Fred, Codes and Cyphers. (2005)
2. Kelly, K.: *What Technology Wants.* (2011)
3. Poster, M: *The Mode of Information.* (1990)
4. Fuller, B.: *Synergetics, Explorations in the Geometry of Thinking.* New York. Macmillan. (1975)
5. Bauman, Z.: *Liquid Modernity.* (2000)
6. Kurzwell, R.: *The Singularity is Near.* (2005)

AETIOLOGY OF A SECURE NETWORK

1. Human Brain Project: European Commission Project. See:
    https://www.humanbrainproject.eu/en_GB. Accessed 10th April 2014.
2. DeRose, S., Bringsjord: *Are Computers Alive*, Abacus, Vol. 2, No. 4, (1985)
    Springer-Verlag, New York, Inc.
3. Turing, A.: *Computing Machinery and Intelligence*. Mind. (1950)
4. Ayer, A.: Language, *Truth and Logic*. (1936)
5. Wittgenstein, L.: *Logisch-Philosophische*. (1921)
6. Wittgenstein, L.: *Tractatus Logico-Philosophicus*. (1922)
7. Kelly, K.: *What Technology Wants*. (2011)
8. Arthur, W.B.: *The Nature of Technology*. (2009)
9. Watson, Richard.: *Future Minds: How the Digital Age is Changing Our Minds, Why this Matters and What We Can Do About It*., (2010)
10. Talbott, Steve.: *The Future Does Not Compute: Transcending the Machines in our Midst*. (1995)
11. Lanier, Jaron.: *Who Owns the Future*, Penguin (2013)

BUILDING ACTOR-COHERENT DEFENCES

12. Plato.: *Collected Dialogues*.
13. Heisenberg, Werner.: *Physics and Philosophy*. (1962)
14. Penrose, Roger. *The Road to Reality: A Complete Guide to the Laws of the Universe*. (2007)
15. Tresch, John.: *The Romantic Machine: Utopian Science and Technology After Napoleon*. (2012)
16. Weizenbaum, J.: *Computer Power and Human Reason*. (1976)
17. Wertheimer, M.: *Productive Thinking*. (1959)

PRIMARY-NETWORK DESIGN

1. Baxi, Upendra.: *The Future of Human Rights*. (2012)
2. Veltman Kim.: *Understanding New Media*. (2006)
3. Nelson, Ted.: *Geeks Baring Gifts*., (2013)
4. Veltman Kim.: *The Alphabet of Life*, (2014)
5. McLuhan, Marshall.: *Understanding Media: The Extensions of Man*.,(1964)
6. McLuhan, Marshall.: *The Global Village: Transformations in World Life and Media in the 21st Century*., (1989)
7. Shannon, Claude, E.: *A Mathematical Theory of Communication*. (1949)
8. *Universal Declaration of Human Rights. UN General Assembly. (1948)*
9. Volokh, Eugene (2000).: *"Freedom of Speech, Information Privacy, and the Troubling Implications of a Right to Stop People from Speaking about You"*. Stanford Law Review 52 (5): 1049–1124. doi:10.2307/1229510.
10. Solove, Daniel J. (2003).: *The Virtues of Knowing Less: Justifying Privacy Protections against Disclosure*. Duke Law Journal 53 (3): 967–1065 [p. 976]. JSTOR 1373222.

11. Mayes, Tessa (18 March 2011): "We have no right to be forgotten online". The Guardian.
12. Mumford, L.: The Myth of the Machine: Volume 1.(1971)

ENCRYPTION THEORY

1. Development: The Myth of the Machine: Volume 1.,(1971)
2. Hofstadter, Douglas, R.: Godel, Escher and Bach: An Eternal Golden Braid.,(1979)
3. Hofstadter, Douglas, R.: Surfaces and Essences. (2013)
4. Aristotelian Society. Men and Machines; Symposia Read at the Joint Session of the Aristotelian Society and the Mind Association at Birmingham (July 11th-13th 1952.) Harrison and Sons Ltd.
5. Berleant, Daniel.: The Human Race to The Future: What could happen—and What to do.,(2014)
6. Stiegler, Bernard.: Technicity.,(2013)
7. Bell, Wendell.: Foundations of Futures Studies (Volumes 1 and 2).,(2004,2010).
8. Lanier, Jaron.: Who Owns the Future, Penguin, (2013)
9. Mitchell, William, J.: Me++; The Cyborg Self and the Networked City., (2003)
10. Baxi, Upendra.: The Future of Human Rights.,(2012)

THE BEHOLDER'S SHARE

1. Laurel, B.: Computers as Theatre., Addison-Wesley Publishing Company Inc. (1991)
2. Sutherland, I.: Sketchpad – A Man Machine Graphical Communication System. AFIPS Conference meeting. (1963)
3. Johnson, J., et al.: The Xerox "Star: A Retrospective". Online Article: http://members.dcn.org/dwnelson/XeroxStarRetrospective.html. Retrieved 2013-08-13.
4. Hiltzik, M.A.: Dealers of Lightening, Zerox PARC and the Dawn of the Computer Age. Harper Collins, New York. (1999)
5. Gombrich, E.: Art and Illusion. Phaidon Press Ltd. (1960)
6. Brand, S.: The Media Lab: Inventing The Future at M.I.T., p. 144. R.R. Donnelley and Sons., USA. (1989)
7. Veltman, K.H.: Linear Perspective and the Visual Dimensions of Science and Art. Deutscher Kunstverlag. (1986)

BIGGER-BRAIN VS STEALTH

1. Kennedy, Barbar, M., Bell, David.: Cybercultures and the World we Live in. The Cybercultures Reader., (2000).
2. Rushkoff, Douglas.: Cyberia: Life in the Trenches of Hyperspace.,(1994).
3. Veltman Kim.: The Alphabet of Life, (2014).
4. Veltman Kim.: Understanding New Media, (2006).
5. Rose, N.: Inventing Ourselves.

6. Prince Philip.: HRH The Duke of Edinburgh. *Men, Machines and Sacred Cows.*,(1982).
7. Berleant, Daniel.: *The Human Race to The Future:What could happen—and What to do.*,(2014).
8. Wells, Herbert, George.: *World Brain.*,(1936).
9. Gaines, Brian, R.: *Convergence to the Information Highway,* (1996).
10. Otlet, Pual. Monde: *Essai d'universalisme,* (1935).
11. Bush, Vannevar.: *As We May Think.* The Atlantic, (1945).
12. Licklider, J.C.R.: *Man-Computer Symbiosis.*,(1960).
13. Rheingold, Howard.: *Tools for Thought.* MIT Press, (1983).
14. Hafner, Katie., Lyon, Matthew.: *Where Wizards Stay Up Late:The Origins of the Internet.*,(1998).
15. Aspray, William.: *Computer:A History of the Information Machine.*, (2004).
16. Barrett, Neil.: *The Binary Revolution:The History and Development of the Computer.*,(2006).
17. Nelson, Ted.: *Possiplex—An Autobiography of Ted Nelson.*, (2011).
18. Buckland, Michael. Emanuel Goldberg and His Knowledge Machine. (2006).

PRIVACY AND SECURITY—THE BIG PICTURE

1. Nelson, Ted.: *Geeks Baring Gifts.*, (2013).
2. Nelson, Ted.: *Computer Lib / Dream Machines,*(1974).
3. Nelson, Ted.: *The Hypertext,* Proceedings of the World Documentation Federation, (1965).
4. Nelson, Ted.: *A File Structure for the Complex, The Changing and the Indeterminate. Complex Information Processing,* proceedings of the ACM 20th national conference 1965, (1965).
5. Nelson, Ted.: *Literary Machines,* (1982).
6. Radley, A.: Computers as Self., Proceedings of the 4th International Conference in Human-Computer Interaction, Tourism and Cultural Heritage, (2013).
7. Veltman, Kim.: *Frontiers in Conceptual Navigation for Cultural Heritage,* (2001).
8. Veltman, Kim.: *Towards a Semantic Web for Culture,* (2004).
9. Veltman, Kim.: *Understanding New Media.*
10. Wells, Herbert, George.: *World Brain.*,(1936).
11. Otlet, Pual.: Monde: *Essai d'universalisme,* (1935).
12. Buckland, Michael. Emanuel Goldberg and His Knowledge Machine. (2006).

A THEORY OF ABSOLUTE SECURITY

1. Woolley, Benjamin.: *Virtual Worlds.*, (1994).
2. Rheingold Howard.: *Virtual Reality.*,(1991).
3. Markley, Robert.: *Virtual Realities and Their Discontents.*,(1995).
4. Blascovich, Jim, Bailenson, Jeremy. *Infinite Reality:Avatars, Eternal Life, New Worlds, and the Dawn of the Virtual Revolution.*,(2011).
5. Artaud, Antonin.: *The Theatre and its Double.*, (1938).
6. Lanham, Richard.: *The Electronic Word.*, (1995).
7. Phillip Rogaway, The Moral Failure of Computer Scientists, The Atlantic, 2016.

Bibliography

Abbott Abott, Edwin.: *Flatland.*(1884).

Anderson, Chris. *Free: The Future of a Radical Price.* New York, (2006).

Anderson, Walter, Truett.: *The Future of the Self.,*(1997).

Aristotelian Society.: *Men and Machines; Symposia Read at the Joint Session of the Aristotelian Society and the Mind Association at Birmingham (July 11th-13th 1952).* Harrison and Sons Ltd.

Aristotle., Barnes, Jonathan.: *The Complete Works of Aristotle; Volumes 1 and 2.,*(1984).

Armand, Louis., Bradley, Arthur., Zizek, Slavoj., Stiegler, Bernard.: *Technicity.,*(2013).

Arnasaon, H.,H., Mansfield, Elizabeth, C.: *A History of Modern Art, 7th Edition.,* (2012).

Arthur, W.B.: *The Nature of Technology.,* (2009).

Ash, Brian.: *The Visual Encyclopaedia of Science Fiction.,* (1978).

Ashby, W.R.: *Introduction to Cybernetics.,*(1956).

Aspray, William.: *Computer: A History of the Information Machine.,* (2004).

Astounding Science Fiction Magazine: 1930s—1980s

Asimov, I.: *I Robot.* (1940-1950)

Asimov, Isaac.: *Machines that Think: The Best Science Fiction Stories About Robots and Computers.,* (1985).

Asimov, Isaac.: *Robot Visions.,* (1991).

Auletta, Ken.: *Googled, The End of the World as We Know It.,* (2011).

Ayer, A.: *Language, Truth and Logic.* (1936)

Banks, Michael, A.: *On the Way to the Web: The Secret History of the Internet and its Founders.,*(2011).

Barrett, Neil.: *The Binary Revolution: The History and Development of the Computer.,*(2006).

Battelle, John.: *Search,* (2006).

Baxi, Upendra.: *The Future of Human Rights.,*(2012).

Baudrillard, J.: *Fatal Strategies.* ,(1983).

Baudrillard, Jean.: *Simulacra and Simulation.,*(1981).

Baudrillard, Jean.: *Simulations.,* (1983).

Bauman, Z.: *Liquid Modernity.* ,(2000).

Bell, Wendell.: *Foundations of Futures Studies (Volumes 1 and 2).,*(2004),(2010).

Berleant, Daniel.: *The Human Race to The Future: What could happen—and What to do.,*(2014).

Berners-Lee, Tim.: *Weaving the Web,* (1999).

Berry, Adrian.: *The Next Ten Thousand Years.,*(1975).

Blascovich, Jim, Bailenson, Jeremy.: *Infinite Reality: Avatars, Eternal Life, New Worlds, and the Dawn of the Virtual Revolution.,*(2011).

Bragdon, Claude, Fayette.: *A Primer of Higher Space (The Fourth Dimension).,*(1923).

Bradbury, Ray.: *Fahrenheit 451.,*(1953).

Brand, Stewart.: *The Clock of the Long Now: Time and Responsibility: The Ideas Behind the World's Slowest Computer.,*(2000).

Brand, S.: *The Media Lab: Inventing The Future at M.I.T.,* p. 144. R.R.Donnelley and Sons., USA.,(1989).

Brate, Adam.: *Technomanifestos:Visions of the Information Revolutionaries.,*(2002).

Brown, Jonathon.: *The Self.,*(2007).

Brunn, Stanely.: *Collapsing Space and Time.,(1991).*

Bolt, Richjard.: *The Human Interface, Where People and Computer Meet.,* (1984).

Boole, George.: *An Investigation into The Laws of Thought.,*(1854).

Bowman, D.A.: *3D User Interfaces, Theory and Practice.* Addision Wesley. ,(2004).

Buckland, Michael. Emanuel Goldberg and His Knowledge Machine. (2006).
   Burdea,George. C., Coiffet, Philippe.:*Virtual Reality Technology.,*(2003).

Bush,Vannevar.: *As We May Think.*The Atlantic, (1945).

Calabrese, Andrew et al.: *Communication, Citizenship and Social Policy.,*(1999).

Cassirer Ernst.: *The Myth of the State.,*(1961).

Cassirer Ernst.: *The Philosophy of Symbolic Forms:Volumes 1-3.,*(1965).

Cassirer, Ernst.: *The Problem of Knowledge: Philosophy, Science and History Since Hegel. (*1969).

Claeys, Gregory., Sargent, Lyman, Tower.: *The Utopia Reader.,*(1999).

Clarke, Arthur, C.: *The Exploration of Space.,*(2010).

Cohen, John.: *Human Robots in Myth and Science.,*(1966).

Cork, Richard.: *Vorticism and Abstract Art in the Machine Age (2 volumes).,*(1976).

Copleston, Frederick.: *A History of Philosophy; volumes 1-11.,* (1946-1974).

Cotton, Bob; Oliver, Richard.: *Understanding Hypermedia.* ,(1983).

Coxeter, H.S.M.: *Introduction to Geometry.,*(1989).

Daily Telegraph.: *Do we want to give them A License to Kill?* (November 15th 2013).

Dale, Rodney.: *Edwardian Inventions.,*(1979).

Dasgupta, S.: *A History of Indian Philosophy.*Volume 1.,(1940).

Dawkins, Richard.: *The Blind Watchmaker.* (1986).

de Bono, Edward.: *Lateral Thinking: An Introduction.,*(1999).

de Bono, Edward.: *The Mechanism of Mind.,(1976).*

de Bono, Edward.: *Eureka.,*(1979).

de La Mettrie, Julien, Offray.: *Man a Machine.,* (1748).

de Sola Pool, Ithiel.: *Technologies of Freedom.,*(1984).

de Vries, Leonard.: *Victorian Inventions.,* (1991).

Debord, Guy.: *Society of the Spectacle.,*(1984)

DeRose, S., Bringsjord:Are Computers Alive? Abacus,Vol. 2, No. 4, (1985). Springer-Verlag, New York, Inc.

Descartes, R.: *Mediations on First Philosophy.,*(1641).

Descartes, R.: *Discourse on the Method of Rightly Conducting the Reason, and Seeking Truth in the Sciences.,*(1637).

Deutsch, David.: *The Fabric of Reality: The Science of Parallel Universes—and Its Implications.*,(1998).

D.H.L Hieronimus, Meyerhoff, Zohara, J.: *The Future of Human Experience: Visionary Thinkers on the Science of Consciousness.*, (2013).

Dick, Philip, K.: *Eye in the Sky.*,(1957).

Dick, Philip, K.: *A Scanner Darkly.*,(1977).

Dick, Philip, K.: *Do Androids Dream of Electric Sheep.*,|(1968).

Dick, Philip, K.: *The Man in the High Castle.*,(1962).

Dick, Philip, K.: *The Minority Report.*,(1956).

Diderot, D.: *Pensees Philosopiques.* (1746)

Domhoff., G.W.: *Wealth, Income and Power.* On-line article: http://www2.ucsc.edu/whorulesamerica/power/wealth.html (accessed 7th April 2014).

Earnshaw, R., A., Gigante, M., A., Jones, H.: *Virtual Reality Systems.*, (1995).

Elliott, Anthony.: *Concepts of the Self.*,(2007).

Encyclopaedia Britannica: 11th Edition, 29th editions.

Ernst, b.: *The Magic Mirror of M.C.Escher.* Taschen GmbH.,(2007).

Engelbart, E.: *Augmenting Human Intellect: A Conceptual Framework.*,(1962).

Flocon, A., Barre, A.: *Curvilinear Perspective, From Visual Space to the Constructed Image.* University of California Press.,(1992).

Fraser, J., Y.: *The Voices of Time.*, (1981).

Frewin, Anthony.: *One Hundred Years of Science Fiction Illustration.*,(1988).

Frauenfelder, Mark. *The Computer: An Illustrated History.*, (2013)

Freud, S.: *The Interpretation of Dreams.* (1899)

Forster, E.M.: *The Machine Stops.*,(1909).

Foucault, Michel.: *Discipline and Punishment: The Birth of the Prison.* Penguin,(1975).

Foucault, Michel.: *The Order of Things: An Archaeology of the Human Sciences.*,(1966).

Fuller, R. Buckminster.: *Operating Manual for Spaceship Earth.*, (1969).

Fuller, Buckminster.: *Synergetics, Explorations in the Geometry of Thinking.* New York. Macmillan.,(1975).

Fuller, R. Buckminster.: *Utopia or Oblivion: The Prospects for Humanity.*,(1972).

Gelernter, David.: *Mirror Worlds: or the Day Software Puts the Universe in a ShoeBox... How it will Happen and What it Will Mean.*,(1993).

George, Frank.: *Man the Machine.*,(1979).

Gibson, J.J.: *Th Ecological Approach to Visual Perception.* Psychology Press. ,(1986).

Gibson, William.: *Neuromancer*, (1984).

Ginsberg, Morris.: *On the Diversity of Morals.*,(1957).

Gleick, James.: *The Information: A History, A Theory, A Flood.*, (2012).

Gabor, D.: *Innovations: Scientific, Technological, and Social.*, (1970).

Gombrich, E.: *Art and Illusion.* Phaidon Press Ltd. (1960)

Gray, Chris, Hables.: *Cyborg Citizen; Politics in the Posthuman Age.*,(2002).

Grau, Oliver.: *Virtual Art.*, (2004).

Grills, Chad.: *Future Proof: Mindsets for 21st Century Success.*, (2014).

Hafner, Katie., Lyon, Matthew.: *Where Wizards Stay Up Late: The Origins of the Internet.*,(1998).

Halacy, D.S.: *Cyborg: Evolution of the Superman.*,(1965).

Hamelink, Cees, J.: *The Ethics of Cyberspace.*,(2000).

Hamit, Francis.: *Virtual Reality and the Exploration of Cyberspace.*, (1993).

Haraway, Donna.J., Hables-Gray, Chris., Eglash, Ron., Clynes, Manfred.E.: *The Cyborg Handbook.*, (1995).

Henderson, Linda, Dalrymple.:*The Fourth Dimension and Non-Euclidean Geometry in Modern Art.*,(1983).

Heppenheimer T.A.: *Colonies in Space.*,(1977).

Heil, John.: *The Nature of True Minds.*,(1992).

Heidegger, Martin.: *Being and Time.*,(1927).

Heidegger, Martin.: *What is Called Thinking?*,(1976).

Heim, Michael. *The Metaphysics of Virtual Reality.*,(1994).

Hertzfeld, Andy.: *Revolution in the Valley*, (2011).

Hiltzik, M.A.: *Dealers of Lightening, Zerox PARC and the Dawn of the Computer Age.* Harper Collins, New York.,(1999).

Hinton, Charles, Howard.: *The Fourth Dimension.*,(1913).

Hobbes, Thomas.: *Leviathan.*,(1668).

Hodges, Andrew., Hofstadter, Douglas.: *Alan Turing: The Enigma.*,(1982).

Hofstadter, Douglas, R.: *Godel, Escher and Bach: An Eternal Golden Braid.*,(1979).

Hofstadter, Douglas, R.: *Surfaces and Essences.*, (2013).

Hofstadter, Douglas, R.: *The Mind's I: Fantasies and Reflections on Self and Soul.*, (1982).

Hofstadter Douglas.: *Metamagical Themas: Questing for the Essence of Mind and Pattern.*, (1986).

Holtzman, Steve, R.: *Digital Mantras: The Language of Abstract and Virtual Worlds.*, (1995).

Howard, I.P, Rogers, B.J.: *Binocular Vision and Stereopsis.* Oxford University Press. (1995)

Howe, Jeff.: *Crowdsourcing: Why the Power of the Crowd is Driving the Future of Business.*, (2009)

Human Brain Project: European Commission Project. See: https://www.humanbrainproject.eu/en_GB. Accessed (10th April 2014).

Hume, David.: *A Treatise on Human Nature.*, (1738).

Hume, Robert, Ernest.: *The Thirteen Principal Upanishads.*, (2010).

Hunger Statistics, United Nations World Food Programme.,(2013).

Husserl, Edmund. *Ideas: A General Introduction to Phenomenology: Volumes 1-3.*,(1913-).

Husserl, Edmund, Gustav, Albrecht.: *Logical Investigations.*, (1900).

Huxley, Aldous.: *Brave New World.*,(1931).

Jacobson, Linda.: *CyberArts: Exploring Art and Technology.*,(1992).

Johnson, George.: *In the Palaces of Memory: How We Build the Worlds Inside Our Heads.*,(1992).

Johnson,J., et al.: *The Xerox "Star:A Retrospective.* Online Article: http://members.dcn.org/dwnelson/XeroxStarRetrospective.html. Retrieved 2013-08-13.

Jarvis, Jeff.: *What Would Google Do?*, (2001).

Jung,C.: *Archetypes and the Collective Unconscious.*,(1959).

Jung, Carl.: *Man and His Symbols*, (1968).

Jung, C.G.,: Hull, R.F.C. *The Collected Works of Carl Jung (Volumes 1-20).*,(1960-1990).

Kant, Immanuel.: *Critique of Pure Reason.*,(1787).

Kahn, David.: *The Code Breakers:The Comprehensive History of Secret Communication from Ancient Times to the Internet.*, (1996).

Kelly, K.: *What Technology Wants.*,(2011).

Kent, Ernest,W.: *The Brains of Men and Machines.*,(1980).

Kery, Patricia, Frantz.: *Art Deco Graphics.*,(1986).

Kirk, G.S., Raven, J.E.:*The Pre-Socratic Philosophers.*,(1969).

Kirkpatrick, David.: *The Facebook Effect:The Inside Story of the Company That is Connecting the World.*,(2011).

Klee, Paul.: *Notebooks of Paul Klee (Volumes 1 and 2)*, (1964, 1992).

Koepsell, David, R.: *The Ontology of Cyberspace: Philosophy, Law and the Future of Intellectual Property.*, (2003).

Krueger, Myron.: *Artificial Reality 2.* (1991).

Kurzweil, Ray.: *The Age of Spiritual Machines:When Computers Exceed Human Intelligence.*,(1999).

Laithwaite, Eric.: *An Inventor in the Garden of Eden.*,(1994).

Lanier, Jaron.: *Who Owns the Future*, Penguin, (2013).

Lanier, Jaron.: *You are Not a Gadget:A Manifesto.*, (2001).

Landauer,Thomas, K.: *The Trouble with Computers: Usefulness, Usability, and Productivity.*,(1996).

Laurel, Brenda.: *The Art of the Human Computer Interface.*, (1990).

Laurel, B.: *Computers as Theatre.* Addison-Wesley Publishing Company Inc., (1991).

Leibniz, Gottfried Wilhelm.: *Philosophical Papers and Letters:Volumes 1 and 2.*, 1976, (2011).

Lemert, C.: *Thinking the Unthinkable,The Riddles of Classical Social Theories.*,(2007).

Lem, Stanislaw.: *The Cyberiad: Fables for the Cybernetic Ward.*, (1976).

Levy, Steven.: *How the NSA nearly destroyed the Internet.* Wired Magazine, January (2014).

Levy, Stephen.: *In the Plex; How Google Things, Works, and Shapes Our Lives.*, (2012).

Lewis,Arthur, O.: *Of Men and Machines.*,(1963).

Licklider, J.C.R.: *Man-Computer Symbiosis.*,(1960).

Lilley, S.: *Men, Machines and History.*, (1948).

Linzmayer, Owen. *Apple Confidential 2.0*, 2004.

Locke, John.: *An Essay Concerning Human Understanding.*,(1689).

Lombardo,Thomas.: *Contemporary Futurist Thought: Science Fiction, Future Studies, and Theories and Visions of the Future in the Last Century.*,(2006).

Lovejoy, Arthur, O.: *The Great Chain of Being: A Study of the History of an Idea.,*(1936).

Lovelock, James.: Gaia.

Lovelock, James.: *A Rough Ride to the Future,*(2014).

Luppicini, Rocci.: *Handbook of Research on Technoself: Identity in a Technological Society.,* (2012).

MacKay, Donald, Information, Mechanism and Meaning, The MIT Press, 1969

Mannheim, Karl.: *Ideology and Utopia: An Introduction to the Sociology of Knowledge.,*(1955).

Markley, Robert.: *Virtual Realities and Their Discontents.,*(1995|).

Markoff, John.: *From Counterculture to Cyberculture: Stewart Brand, the Whole Earth Network and the Rise of Digital Utopianism.,* (2008).

Markoff, John.: *What the Dormouse Said: How the Sixties Counterculture Shaped the Personal Computer Industry.,*(2006).

Marx, Carl., Engels, Friedrich.: *The Communist Manifesto.,*(1848).

Marx, K.: *Das Kapital.,*(1867).

Maslow, A.: *Motivation and Personality.,*(1954).

Merleau-Ponty, Maurice.: *Signs.,* (1964).

Merleau-Ponty, Maurice.: *Nature.,*(2000).

Menezes, ALfred, J., von Oorschot, Paul, C., Vanstobe, Scott, A.: *Handbook of Applied Cryptography.,*(1996).

McLuhan, Marshall.: *The Mechanical Bride: Folklore of Industrial Man.,* (1967).

McLuhan, Marshall.: *Understanding Media: The Extensions of Man.,*(1964).

McLuhan, Marshall.: *The Global Village: Transformations in World Life and Media in the 21st Century.,* (1989).

Mill, John, Stuart.: *On Liberty.,* (1859).

Mitchell, WIlliam. J.: *e-topia.,*(2000).

Mitchell, William, J.: *Me++; The Cyborg Self and the Networked City.,* (2003).

Moore, G., E.: *Principia Ethica.,*(1966).

More, Max., Vita-More, Natasha.: *The Transhumanist Reader: Classical and Contemporary Essays on the Science, Technology and Philosophy of the Human Future.,*(2013).

More, Thomas.: *Utopia.,* (1516).

Moritz, Michael.: *Return to the Little Kingdom: Steve Jobs and the Creation of Apple.,* (2010).

Morrison, E.: *Men, Machines and Modern Times.,*(1966).

Mudrick, Marvin.: *The Man in the Machine.,* (1977).

Muller, Max.: *Sacred Books of the East: The Texts of Taoism.,* (1891).

Mumford, Lewis.: *The Pentagon of Power: The Myth of the Machine.,*(1970).

Mumford, Lewis.: *Technics and Human Development: The Myth of the Machine: Volume 1.,*(1971).

Murrell, Hywel.: *Men and Machines.,*(1976).

Nagel, Ernest.: *The Structure of Science.,*(1961).

Nelson, Ted.: *Computer Lib / Dream Machines,*(1974).

Nelson, Ted.: *Geeks Baring Gifts.,* (2013).

Nelson, Ted.: *Possiplex—An Autobiography of Ted Nelson.,* (2011).

Nietzsche, F.: *The Wanderer and his Shadow.*,(1880).
Nietzsche, F.: *Daybreak.*,(1880).
Nietzsche, F.: *Thus spoke Zarathustra.*,(1883).
Norman, Donald, A.: *The Invisible Computer.*, (1999).

O'Brien, Fitz, James.: *The Diamond Lens.*,(1858).
O-Neill, Gerard, K.: *2081: A Hopeful View of the Human Future.*, (1981).
Omni Magazine: Complete Collection
Orwell, George.: *Animal Farm.* ,(1949).
Orwell, George.: *Nineteen Eight-Four.* Secker and Warburg, London, (1949).
Otlet, Pual.: Monde: *Essai d'universalisme,* (1935).
Ouspensky , P.D.: *A New Model of the Universe.*,(1969).
Ouspensky , P.D.: *In Search of the Miraculous.*, (1949).

Panofsky, E.: *Perspective as a symbolic form.* Zone Books. (1997)
Penrose, Roger.: *The Road to Reality: A Complete Guide to the Laws of the Universe.*,(2007).
Pinker, Steven.: *How the Mind Works.*,(2009).
Pinker, Steven.: *The Stuff of Thought: Language as a Window into Human Nature.*, (2008).
Plato.: Collected Dialogues.
Plato.: Cornford, Franics.,M. *Plato's Theory of Knowledge: The Theaetetus and The Sophist Plato.*,(1957).
Ploman, Edward, W., Hamilton, L. Clark.: *Copyright: Intellectual Property in the Information Age.*,(1980).
Popper, Karl, J.: *The Open Society and It's Enemies (Volume 1 and 2).*,(1971).
Portola Institute.: *The Whole Earth Catalogue.*, (1972) Edition, (1986) Edition, (1995) Edition.
Poster, M: *The Mode of Information.*,(1990).
Prince Philip.: HRH The Duke of Edinburgh. *Men, Machines and Sacred Cows.*,(1982).

Radhakrishnan, S., Raju, P.,T.: *The Concept of Man: A Study in Comparative Philosophy.*, (1960).
Radley, A.S.: *Mirror System Producing a Real Space 3-D Reflected Image of a Person (Hologram Mirror).* UK Patent granted—GB2454763.,(2009).
Radley, A.: Self as Computer—2015.
Radley, A.: Humans versus Computers Systems and Machines; a Battle for Freedom, Equality and Democracy, keynote paper, Proceedings of the 6th International Conference in Human-Computer Interaction, Tourism and Cultural Heritage, (2015).
Rand, Ayn.: *Atlas Shrugged.*,(1957).
Rand, Ayn.: *The Fountainhead.*,(1943).
Reichardt, Jasia.: *Robots: Fact, Fiction and Prediction.*,(1978).
Rheingold, Howard.: *Tools for Thought.* MIT Press, (1983).
Rheingold Howard.: *Virtual Reality.*,(1991).
Roberts, Keith.: *Machines and Men.*,(1973).

Rogers, Everett M.: *Diffusion of Innovations.* (2003).

Roheim , Geza,. Muensterberger, Warner,; Magic and Schizophrenia., (2006).

Rogaway, Pillip, The Moral Failure of Computer Scientists, The Atlantic, 2016

Rose, N.: *Governing the Soul.*

Rose, N.: *Inventing Ourselves.*

Ross, K.W., Kurose, James, F.: *Computer Networking;   A Top Down Approach.,* (2012).

Roszak, Theodore.: *The Making of a Counter Culture.,* (1969).

Routledge, Robert.: *Discoveries and Inventions of the 19th Century.,* (1900).

Rucker, Rudy.: *Mind Tools.* Penguin Books, (1987).

Rucker, Rudolf., Povilaitis, David.: *The Fourth Dimension: A Guided Tour of the Universe.,* (1985).

Rushkoff, Douglas.: *Cyberia: Life in the Trenches of Hyperspace.,* (1994).

Russell, Bertrand.: *Skeptical Essays.* Unwin Hyman Ltd,(1963).

Russell, Bertrand.: *The Problems of Philosophy.,* (1912).

Sagan Carl.: *Dragons of Eden: Speculations on the Evolution of Human Intelligence.,* (1986).

Sagan, C.: *The Demon Haunted World: Science as a Candle in the Dark.,* (1997).

Salinger. J.: *The Catcher in the Rye.,* (1951).

Salomon, David., Bryant, D.: *Handbook of Data Compression.,* (2009).

Sartre, Jean-Paul.: *Imagination.,* (1962).

Sartre, Jean-Paul.: *Being and Nothingness: An Essay on Phenomenological Ontology.,* (1943).

Shelley, Mary.: *Frankenstein, or The Modern Prometheus.* (1818).

Schopenhauer, A.: *The World As Will and Representation.,* (1844).

Searle, John, R. :*The Mystery of Consciousness.,* (1990).

Shannon, Claude, E.: *A Mathematical Theory of Communication.* (1949).

Shannon, Claude, E.: Theory of Secret Systems.

Singleton, W., T.: *Man-Machine Systems.,* (1974).

Sutherland, I.: *Sketchpad; A Man Machine Graphical Communication System.* AFIPS Conference meeting,(1963).

Talbott, Steve.: *The Future Does Not Compute: Transcending the Machines in our Midst.* (1995).

Tanenbaum, Andrew, S., Wetherall, David.J.: *Computer Networks (5th Edition).,*(2010).

Thring, M.W.: *Man, Machines and Tomorrow.,* (1973).

Toffler, Alvin.: *Future Shock.,* (1984).

Tresch, John.: *The Romantic Machine: Utopian Science and Technology After Napoleon.,* (2012).

Tuck, M.: *The Real History of the GUI.* Online article: http://www.sitepoint.com/real-history-gui/. Retrieved (2013-08-13).

Tufte, Edward.: *Envisioning Information.,* (1990).

Tufte, Edward.: *The Visual Display of Quantitive Information.,* (2001).

Turkle, Sherry.: *The Second Self: Computers and the Human Spirit.*, (1984).
Turing, A.: *Computing Machinery and Intelligence.* Mind. (1950).

UK Patent Office Abridgements of Specifications: (1900-1901, 1904, 1925).
Universal Declaration of Human Rights. UN General Assembly. (1948).

Veltman Kim.: *The Alphabets of Life*, (2014).
Veltman Kim.: *Understanding New Media*, (2006).
Veltman, K.H.: *Linear Perspective and the Visual Dimensions of Science and Art.*
   Deutscher Kunstverlag,(1986). (http://vmmi.sumscorp.com)
Veltman, K.H.: *Bibliography of Perspective.*   *(1975-1995).* See online version :
   http://vmmi.sumscorp.com/develop/
Veltman, K.H.: *Sources of Perspective; Literature of Perspective (1985-1995);* See
   online: http://sumscorp.com/perspective/
Verne, Jules.: *Twenty Thousand Leagues Under the Sea.*,(1870).
von Helmholtz, Hermann.: *A Treatise on Physiological Optics*
   (Volumes 1-3)., (1910).

Watson, Richard.: *Future Minds: How the Digital Age is Changing Our Minds, Why*
   this Matters and What We Can Do About It., (2010).
Wells, Herbert, George.: *First and Last Things.*,(1908).
Wells, Herbert, George.: *The Shape of Things to Come.*,(1933).
Wells, Herbert, George.: *A Modern Utopia.*,(1905).
Wells, Herbert, George.: *World Brain.*,(1936).
Wertheimer, Max.: *Productive Thinking.* (1971)
Whitehead, Alfred, North.: *Process and Reality.*,(1929).
Wiener, Norman.: *God and Golem: Comments on Certain Points Where*
   Cybernetics Impinges on Religion., (1990).
Wilhelm, Richard.: *The Secret of the Golden Flower: A Chinese Book*
   of Life.,(1945).
Wired Magazine: Complete Collection
Wittgenstien, L.: *Logisch-Philosophische.* ,(1921).
Wittgenstein, Ludwig.: *Philosophical Grammar.*, (1969).
Wittgenstien, L.: *Tractatus Logico-Philosophicus.* ,(1922).
Wolfram, Stephen.: *A New Kind of Science.*,(2002).
Woolley, Benjamin.: *Virtual Worlds.*, (1994).
Wurman, Saul.: *Information Anxiety.*, (1989).
Wurster, Christian.: *Computers: An Illustrated   History.*, (2002).

Yates, Francis.: *The Art of Memory.*,(2001).

Zamyatin, Yevgeny., Brown, Clarence.: *We.,(1921).*
Zittrain, Jonathan.: *The Future of the Internet: And How to Stop It.*, (2009).

Appendix A

Security System Characterisation

EVIDENTLY, we have three <u>legitimate</u> kinds of accessibility or *Privacy Status* (secret, private, open)—associated with three types of *Access Protection* (owner-restricted, single-copy-send, universal-send/receive).

Established is that, communications security—or protection of social accessibility status—is a time-bound property that must be provided by relevant security mechanism(s)—specifically:

Carefully designed human or manual working procedures (i.e. particular social structures, regulated human-human interaction(s), prescribed data communication events/formats, specific social processes etc); and also by means of:

Adequately secure automatic and semi-automatic systems—or the locking, blocking and concealment of primary, secondary, and tertiary network: system access gateway(s)/attack-surfaces.

Overall, security—or access protection—equates to management of a datum-copy's form/content—existing on media of access, storage and transfer. Specifically, by one of the three methods identified: *owner/user-restriction*, *single-copy-send*, and *universal-send/receive*.

The primary aim of security is to prevent **legitimate** secret-datums from morphing into **illegitimate** private-datums or open-datums; and also to prevent legitimate private-datums from morphing onto illegitimate open-datums.

Finally, legitimate open-datum access must be rendered generally accessible—whereby one seeks to protect accessibility for anyone/everyone (ref. open-publication—see the companion book 'Self as Computer / World Brain'). Now that we have developed a comprehensive definition of security, it is necessary to examine the environment(s) in which any particular datum-copy resides.

Typically present are five *Fundamental Categories of Computing Operation(s)* as follows:

- **PROCESSING**—deals with aspects of data: entry, gathering, movement, combination and transformation (local/remote);

- **STORAGE**—deals with aspects of data permanence (local/remote);

- **PRESENTATION**—deals with aspects of data connection, visibility and display (local/remote);

- **COMMUNICATION**—deals with aspects of data transfer.

- **COMMAND AND CONTROL**—deals with aspects of the automatic and semi-automatic control of networked devices (systems/mechanisms) and/or computers (local/remote).

Now for each of the five types of computer operation; a legitimate copy may be either A) secret; B) private or C) open. Ergo, there are (at least) *fifteen different kinds of protective techniques* (or sub-system(s)) that may be required for any particular information security system (see Appendix A). For example: secret and private items on a communication system—often require two different kinds of protection (however both may use some of the same techniques).

Appendix B

Processing Atomicity / Complexity

NETWORKED computers (in general) have advanced to the stage where they are—quite literally—beyond the (complete) understanding of any single human, or even a large organisation of humans. Our degree of personal familiarity with and/or localised knowledge of—all of the vast multitude(s) of low-level implementation details (and their combined/aggregated effects for a particular data-processing path) may be very small/non-existent.

And so we must **take it on faith**—that the top-level 'marketing' promises of what these (potentially) boundless processing units do—is (always) identical to what is claimed for them. But it may often be the case—that even the designers cannot foresee how the individual processing units will work in reality—and/or what will be the precise outcomes of there operation in any specific use-case scenario.

We have processor 'chips' containing billions of components, working on computers containing hundreds of millions of lines of code—code that exists inside many different kinds of programs (that may or may not be running on the same device simultaneously—and often sharing memory and system resources etc). Plus we often have remote-actors (humans, programs) using networked machines and influencing local events and processes etc; and everything connected to hundreds of millions of other networked computers etc.

These complexities and fragmentary logic paths—render into a fiction the atomicity of personal computers, device(s), programming operation(s) etc.

What to do? Perhaps only to—combat lack-of-knowledge/uncertainty—with constant data-gathering, knowledge acquisition etc; and by employing specific monitoring system(s)—both automatic and human types. Plus by reading related news stories, and by staying up-to-date on the latest security exploits/defence-techniques/reports/surveys etc. Good luck!

* * * * *

Appendix C

Countermeasure Solutions

SCF Framework (Communications Domain)

Table of Threats / Protective-Measures

SCF Threat Class	Hacking Target(s)	System Gateway(s)	Effective Countermeasures
1 - Primary Network	-	-	-
1.1 - Access Media	-	-	-
1.1.1 - Local Device	Hacking of locally held Datums.	-	-
1.1.1.1 - Local Data Exploit	Primary-Copy or Secondary-Copy Datum read (r), write (w), execute (x) access (one or more). Example: PC in-situ hacking.	Physical, Virtual, Meaning (local access).	STRATEGY: Lock/Block/Conceal one or more Gateway(s). METHODS: [1] Physical device security. [2] Virtual data security + Meaning Gateway(s) protection. [3] Entry locks on: A) Device, B) Logins, C) Datum Meaning.

SCF Threat Class	Hacking Target(s)	System Gateway(s)	Effective Countermeasures
1.1.1.2 - Remote Sourced Local Data Exploit	Primary-Copy or Secondary-Copy Datum read (r), write (w), execute (x) access (one or more). Example(s): A) PC has worm / virus, B) PC/Data-processing -system has failure in Actor Coherence/Integrit, and/or C) the local network is compromised.	Physical, Virtual, Meaning (remote access).	STRATEGY: Lock/Block/Conceal - Gateway(s). METHODS: [1] Network Security / Firewalls. [2] Virtual data security + Meaning Gateway(s) protection. [3] Entry locks on: A) Logins, B) Datum Meaning. [4] Certify/Qualify: Actor Coherence/Integrity.
1.1.1.3 - Device Replication (Local Source)	A) Device Exploit. B) Primary-Copy or Secondary-Copy Datum read (r), write (w), execute (x) access (one or more).. Example: PC in-situ device replication.	Physical, Virtual (local access).	STRATEGY: Lock/Block/Conceal - Gateway(s). METHODS: [1] Physical device security. [2] Virtual data security + Meaning Gateway(s) protection. [3] Entry locks on: A) Logins, B) Datum Meaning.

SCF Threat Class	Hacking Target(s)	System Gateway(s)	Effective Countermeasures
1.1.1.4 - Device Replication (Remote Source)	A) Device Exploit. B) Primary-Copy or Secondary-Copy Datum read (r), write (w), execute (x) access (one or more). Example: PC remote access device replication.	Virtual, Meaning (remote access).	STRATEGY: Lock/Block/Conceal - Gateway(s). METHODS: [1] Network security / firewalls. [2] Virtual data security + Meaning Gateway(s) protection. [3] Entry locks on: A) Logins, B) Datum Meaning. [4] Certify/Qualify: Actor Coherence/Integrity.
1.1.2 - Access Node	Locally held Datums.	-	-

SCF Threat Class	Hacking Target(s)	System Gateway(s)	Effective Countermeasures
1.1.2.1 - Local Data Storage Exploit (Front-Door)	Exploit for data held locally, access/exploit happens via Central-Server Network and/or network / ID spoofing etc. Primary-Copy or Secondary-Copy Datum read (r), write (w), execute (x) access (one or more). Example: False User ID login Terminal in-situ hacking.	Physical, Virtual, Meaning (local access).	STRATEGY: Lock/Block/Conceal - Gateway(s). METHODS: [1] Physical device security. [2] Virtual data security + Meaning Gateway(s) protection. [3] Entry locks on: A) Logins, B) Datum Meaning. [4] Avoid central copies and data-persistence, employ P2P packet transportation + Single-Copy-Send.

SCF Threat Class	Hacking Target(s)	System Gateway(r)	Effective Countermeasures
1.1.2.1 - Local Data Storage Exploit (Back Door)	Exploit for data held Locally, access/exploit happens via Central-Server Network and/or network / ID spoofing etc and/or corrupt system admin. Primary-Copy or Secondary-Copy Datum read (r), write (w), execute (x) access (one or more). Example: Login Terminal system administrator hacking.	Physical, Virtual, Meaning (local access).	STRATEGY: Lock/Block/Conceal - Gateway(s). METHODS: [1] Physical device security. [2] Virtual data security + Meaning Gateway(s) protection. [3] Entry locks on: A) Device, B) Logins, C) Datum meaning. [4] Avoid central copies and data-persistence, use P2P transport + Single-Copy-Send. [5] Lock-out system-admins from private data by some method.
1.1.3 - Access Node (centrally held Datums)	-	-	-

SCF Threat Class	Hacking Target(s)	System Gateway(s)	Effective Countermeasures
1.1.3.1 - Remote Data Exploit (Front-Door)	Primary-Copy or Secondary-Copy Datum read (r), write (w), execute (x) access (one or more). Example: Login Terminal remote Entrance Gateway hacking; using hacked User ID	Physical, Virtual, Meaning (local access).	STRATEGY: Lock/Block/Conceal - Gateway(s). METHODS: [1] Network security / firewalls. [2] Virtual data security + Meaning Gateway(s) protection. [3] Entry locks on: A) Logins, B) Datum Meaning. [4] Use Peer-To-Peer and Single-Copy-Send techniques to avoid Central_Server Datum Copies and avoid data-persistence.

APPENDIX

SCF Threat Class	Hacking Target(s)	System Gateway(s)	Effective Countermeasures
1.1.3.2 - Remote Data Exploit (Back Door)	Primary-Copy or Secondary-Copy Datum read (r), write (w), execute (x) access (one or more). Example: Central Server System-Admin Login Terminal hacking.	Physical, Virtual, Meaning (local access).	STRATEGY: Lock/Block/Conceal - Gateway(s). METHODS: [1] Physical + Network device security. [2] Virtual data security + Meaning Gateway(s) protection. [3] Entry locks on: A) Device; B) Logins and C) Datum Meaning. [4] Use Peer-To-Peer and Single-Copy-Send techniques to avoid Central_Server Datum Copies and avoid data-persistence.
1.2 - Storage Media	As above	As above	As above
1.3 - Communication Media	-	-	-
1.3.1 - Transfer Media	-	-	-

SCF Threat Class	Hacking Target(s)	System Gateway(s)	Effective Countermeasures
1.3.1.1 - Internal Data Communications Exploit (i.e. Internal network break-ins etc)	Primary-Copy or Secondary-Copy Datum read (r), write (w), execute (x) access (one or more). Example: Data-Breach on Internal network - via worm / virus / network hacking etc.	Physical, Virtual, Meaning (local access).	STRATEGY: Lock/Block/Conceal - Gateway(s). Physical + Network device(s) and Data Communications security measures. METHODS: [1] Methods to prevent IP address routing problems / Spoofing of MAC Address, qualification of IP Node. [2] Virtual entry locks / blocks / concealment on communications data. Meaning Gateway protections on private data. [3] Employ advanced network security methods; including: A) Stealth; B) Invitation Only and Secret Networks; C) Cypher Matching techniques to validate packet destination(s). [4] Network security measures (firewalls etc) to prevent communications break-ins.

SCF Threat Class	Hacking Target(s)	System Gateway(s)	Effective Countermeasures
1.3.1.2 - External Open-Network Data Communications Exploit (i.e. Provider Exploit).	Primary-Copy or Secondary-Copy

Datum read (r).

[Example: Data-Breach on Provider Network or remote false IP address etc.] | Physical, Virtual, Meaning (local access). | STRATEGY:

Lock/Block/Conceal - Gateway(s).

METHODS:

(See above 1.3.1.1 for effective countermeasure techniques)

[1] Use Peer-To-Peer and Single-Copy-Send techniques to avoid Central_Server data persistence and replication of Datum Copies.

[2] Reduce time-of-flight for datum-copies during transportation to reduce likelihood of exploit.

[3] Locking, Blocking, Concealment of packet data. |
| 1.4 - User Identity Management System (UIMS) | - | - | - |
| 1.4.1 - User Identity Exploit | - | - | - |

SCF Threat Class	Hacking Target(s)	System Gateway(s)	Effective Countermeasures
1.4.1.1 - Media Access on UIMS (Physical, Virtual Meaning Gateway exploit(s).	User Identity. False user identity assignment. [Example: remote UIMS break-in / hacking exploit].	Physical, Virtual, Meaning (remote access).	STRATEGY: Lock / Block / Conceal All UIMS Physical / Virtual / Meaning Gateways. > Unique User ID assignment. METHODS: Multiple methods to aid accurate UIMS procedures. [1] Secure UIMS Media/Logins [2] Secure User Information. [3] Secure Encryption Keys. [4] Secure all Access Nodes / Devices. [5] Multiple part ID. [6] Physical ID. [7] Secure passwords. [8] Multi-step Logins. [9] Avoid storing Keys, User IDs on 3rd party servers, rely on PGP methods to identify destination party.

SCF Threat Class	Hacking Target(s)	System Gateway(s)	Effective Countermeasures
1.4.1.2 - **Access Device User Identity Management System Exploit.** (Example is compromised UIMS Access computer)	User Identity. False user identity assignment. UIMS Access Identity > User Identity. False user identity or entry and/or assignment.	Physical, Virtual, Meaning (remote access).	STRATEGY: Multiple methods. Lock / Block / Conceal All UIMS Physical / Virtual / Meaning Gateways. Secure UIMS Media/Devices + related networks. Secure Access Nodes. METHODS: [1] Multiple part ID. [2] Physical ID. [3] Secure passwords. [4] Multi-step Logins. [5] Avoid storing Keys, User IDs on 3rd party servers, rely on PGP methods to identify destination party.

SCF Threat Class	Hacking Target(s)	System Gateway(s)	Effective Countermeasures
1.4.1.3 - **Access Node User Identity Management System Exploit.** (example is stolen / compromised: User ID / encryption keys etc)	1) False Access Node identity assignment 2) False user identity or entry and/or assignment 3) Encryption Keys are broken-into / compromised.	Physical, Virtual, Meaning (remote access).	STRATEGY: Multiple methods. Lock / Block / Conceal All UIMS Physical / Virtual / Meaning Gateways. Secure UIMS Media / Logins. METHODS: [1] Secure Access Nodes / Devices. [2] Multiple part ID. [3] Physical ID. [4] Secure passwords. [5] Multi-step Logins. [6] Local Key Assignment / storage. [7] Hybrid Encryption methods. [8] Avoid storing Keys, User IDs on 3rd party servers, rely on PGP methods to identify destination party.
2. Secondary Network(s)	All of [1] Above.	All of [1] Above.	All of [1] Above.
3. Tertiary Network(s)	All of [1] Above.	All of [1] Above.	All of [1] Above.
4. Replication Network(s)	All of [1] Above.	All of [1] Above.	All of [1] Above.

APPENDIX

SCF Threat Class	Hacking Target(s)	System Gateway(s)	Effective Countermeasures
5. Transmissions Hacking.	Information extraction using communications exploit by means of bulk-data channel funnel from transatlantic cable (for example).	All of [1.3] Above.	All of [1.3] Above.

< END OF CYBERSECURITY THREAT-TABLE >

****

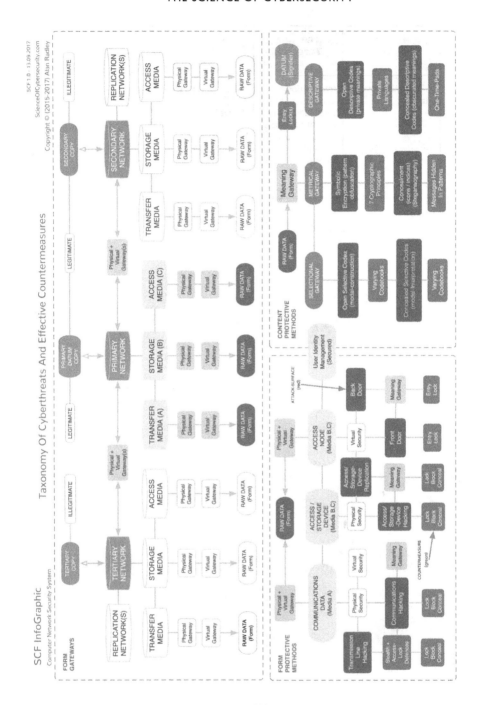

SCF InfoGraphic — Taxonomy Of Cyberthreats And Effective Countermeasures

Computer Network Security System

SCF 1.0 - 13.09.2017
ScienceOfCybersecurity.com
Copyright © (2015-2017) Alan Radley

Appendix D

Cybersecurity Exploit Potential

AS STATED, communications security is protection of access to an item—or datum of meaning.

Wherein access (social form) is defined as the ability of an actor to see/find/contact, open/know and/or change/edit/use an item. As explained, we found that on a network computer—security—is all about protecting copies of datums—whereby we can have three possible types named as **Primary**, **Secondary** and **Tertiary Copies**.

Assumed has been that we are (typically) protecting a private/secret-datum which is to be securely communicated from one party to another.

In other words, we are dealing with the case whereby one wishes to maintain restricted social access to a datum; being a status that must be preserved/defended; and so we wish to avoid instances of an unwarranted party being able to make an illegitimate copy of said datum and/or to open up the inner contents of this item to extract meaning.

It is salient to picture a generalised hacking procedure.

In order to break-into a network security system, a 'hacker' must obtain access to a primary, secondary or tertiary copy—existing on a **Primary**, **Secondary** or **Tertiary Network**. In order to do so, the intruder must first contact with the copy's **FORM** on a related media of **Storage**, **Transfer** or **Access**—existing within the boundaries of said network.

Next the intruder must traverse (pass-through) this same **Physical Gateway**, before opening a **Virtual Gateway** to obtain an intact copy of the datum in its raw form.

Next in order to open up the datum-copy's inner meaning (**CONTENT**) all existing **Meaning Gateway(s)** must be opened (in the correct order)—being of the **Metrical**, **Selectional** and **Descriptive** types.

Ergo—it is important to realise, that for any party to gain access to a protected datum-copy; then all of these steps—Physical Gateway, Virtual Gateway and Meaning Gateway(s) must be successfully traversed for a successful 'exploit' or 'hack'. Note that accordingly—each **Attack Surface** in question is normally defended by some means (basically by **locking**, **blocking** or **concealing** the gateway in question). QED.

Now within the boundaries of this logical analysis—it is possible to develop a taxonomy of all the different types of Cyber-threats that are possible in a nominal network communications security system. Accordingly, we have listed all possible classes of Cyber-threats in Appendix C: Table of Threats and Protective Measures; and also in the related figure in Appendix D: Taxonomy of Cyber-Threats and Effective Countermeasures. We note that these Appendices (C, D & E); provide a useful summary of the theoretical work laid out in the present book.

Another way of assessing security system vulnerability; is in the form of a single equation; named as the **Cybersecurity Exploit Potential**. Such an analysis provides a neat quantitive measure of the likelihood of a nominal Cybersecurity system being 'hacked'; whilst offering a useful starting point from which to begin a more detailed security analysis of any real-world system.

Cybersecurity Exploit Potential (Equation Form)

Computer / Application / Networked System (typical) =

Primary-Network + Secondary-Network(s) + Tertiary-Network(s)—(A)

Total number of datum-copies held on a single network:

N (media) = sum total of all media copies (permanent/transitory) =

N (Transfer Media) + N (Storage Media) + N (Access Media)—(B)

Total number of datum-copies on all networks (single system):

N (total) = sum total of all copies, for all networks, on all media =

N (Primary) [N (transfer) + N (storage) + N (access)] +

N (Secondary(s)) [N (transfer) + N (storage) + N (access)] +

N (Tertiary(s)) [N (transfer) + N (storage) + N (access)] —(C)

Access Pathway: AP [for a single datum held on a single media]:

Actor must traverse a specific pathway to access a datum-copy.

AP = Physical Gateway(s) + Virtual Gateway(s) + Meaning Gateway(s)—(D)

Total Number of Access Pathway(s) for all datum-copies:
Integral property (summed across all media) for a specific time-period:

N (AP) = Integral of all possible Access Pathway(s) for all copies (all networks):

N (AP) = AP (total) * N (total)—(E)

< --- N (AP) units = integer, typically in range dozens-hundreds/thousands. --- >

Exploit Potential (Integral of potential copy exposure events for time-period):

EP (total) = N (AP) * UP (fractional percentage of unprotected AP(s))—(F)

< --- EP units = integer, rounded up. EQUALS ZERO for Absolute Security. --- >

www.ingramcontent.com/pod-product-compliance
Lightning Source LLC
Chambersburg PA
CBHW070944050326
40689CB00014B/3341